STRATEGIC INTERACTION AND MARKETS

STRATEGIC INTERACTION AND MARKETS

JEAN J. GABSZEWICZ

OXFORD
UNIVERSITY PRESS

OXFORD
UNIVERSITY PRESS

Great Clarendon Street, Oxford OX2 6DP

Oxford University Press is a department of the University of Oxford.
It furthers the University's objective of excellence in research, scholarship,
and education by publishing worldwide in

Oxford New York

Athens Auckland Bangkok Bogotá Buenos Aires Calcutta
Cape Town Chennai Dar es Salaam Delhi Florence Hong Kong Istanbul
Karachi Kuala Lumpur Madrid Melbourne Mexico City Mumbai
Nairobi Paris São Paulo Singapore Taipei Tokyo Toronto Warsaw

and associated companies in Berlin Ibadan

Oxford is a registered trade mark of Oxford University Press
in the UK and certain other countries

Published in the United States
by Oxford University Press Inc., New York

British Library Cataloguing in Publication Data

Data available

Library of Congress Cataloging in Publication Data

Data available

ISBN 0–19–823341–8

1 3 5 7 9 10 8 6 4 2

Typeset by The Author
Printed by Biddles Ltd., Guildford and King's Lynn

CONTENTS

1

INTRODUCTION

A perfectly competitive market is defined by four conditions which guarantee
that economic agents operate without any conscious strategic interaction among
themselves. The first condition requires the number of buyers and sellers to be
very large; then no operator might hope to influence the price at which transactions take place. The second condition imposes the absence of any entry barrier
to potential buyers or sellers; as a consequence, the number of operators on the
market can increase as long as a potential buyer or a potential seller has an interest in becoming an effective operator. Free entry of new competitors guarantees
that the number of market operators increases. The third condition stipulates
that the good exchanged should be perfectly homogeneous. From this it follows that products supplied by different sellers are perfect substitutes, so that
all transactions are performed at the same price. Finally, the fourth condition
guarantees that all agents have full information on the distribution of prices announced by the sellers. It then appears impossible for different prices to coexist
on the market: if all prices were not equal, perfect information of buyers would
imply that all of them would wish to buy from the seller setting the lowest price;
in view of gaining some customers, its competitors would then be constrained to
drop their price to the same level. These are the conditions defining a perfectly
competitive market.

When teaching microeconomics, it is not an easy task to illustrate the above
conditions by finding the example of a market which would fulfil all of them
simultaneously. For, no matter which example it is, one or several of these conditions seem to be violated. Could there be a market where buyers and sellers
are so numerous that none of them could imagine influencing the price by his
own individual action? No doubt, an isolated customer would never dispute the
price advertised at some petrol station. But petrol stations which are close to
each other often enter into severe price wars, revealing thereby that prices constitute a crucial strategic weapon for them. In most markets it is observed that
incumbent firms use barriers as a means of preventing the entry of competitors,
for example buying new firms before they start to be operational or occupying
any market niche which might later be chosen by a potential entrant. Which are
the markets where the product sold is fully homogeneous? And even if this were
the case, the simple fact that the product is sold in different shops provides each
shopkeeper a local market power with respect to the customers who are closer
to him than to his competitors. Finally, it is observed everywhere that different
units of the same good are often sold at different prices, whereas the assumption

of perfect information should banish such price differences.

Accordingly, perfect competition is a *cas d'école* which is rarely observed in real market situations. Far from being strategically 'isolated', economic agents seem on the contrary to behave in a way which is the most advantageous to them from the viewpoint of their strategic interaction. We shall see later that the competitive paradigm, in spite of its inadequacy with respect to the observed facts, is still a lively concept among the corporation of microeconomists. This is essentially due to the *normative* properties of perfect competition: while pursuing their private interests as price-takers, economic agents spontaneously realize their collective advantage.

Traditional microeconomic theory is entirely rooted in the competitive framework, and the theory of competitive equilibrium is now viewed as an undisputed pillar of economic theory. An elegant presentation of this theory can be found in Debreu (1959). For a long time, however, economists have devoted a good deal of their efforts to the analysis of market power phenomena, because it has not escaped them that these phenomena are present in most market relations. As long ago as 1838, A.A. Cournot (1838) pioneered a theory explaining price and quantity formation in a regime of *monopoly* and *oligopoly*. These are market contexts in which the competitive assumption, according to which both buyers and sellers are numerous, is no longer satisfied. On the contrary, in these situations the number of sellers is small, and each one of them is conscious of the interactive decision context in which he is involved with his rivals. When choosing the quantity he sends to the market for sale, each seller not only decides about his own level of profits, but also influences the profits of his competitors, via the influence his supply exerts on the selling price. Furthermore, Cournot showed how perfect competition emerges as a limit case of his theory when the number of sellers increases without limit. Each then progressively looses his power to manipulate the selling price, since his individual supply becomes arbitrarily small compared with the aggregate supply. Half a century later, Bertrand (1883) criticized the approach followed by Cournot, with its analysis of *quantity* competition, and proposed instead a similar approach, but relying now on *price* rivalry. He showed that, in the case of a perfectly homogeneous product, price competition leads to the competitive outcome even when only two sellers are present. This follows from the price war which develops between sellers as a consequence of their strategic behaviour.

At the same period, the British economist F.Y. Edgeworth (1881) proposed an exchange model for solving the problem of *bilateral monopoly*, in which two agents exchange the goods they own initially. The notion of the 'contract curve' was defined as the locus of trade outcomes based on a minimal collective rationality assumption, according to which an outcome will not be accepted by traders if there exists another exchange scenario leaving both parties better off. Furthermore, Edgeworth extended his theory to the case of *multilateral exchange*. Then he showed that increasing the number of contracting parties without limit shrinks the contract curve to the set of competitive allocations of the goods. Accordingly his method, like that proposed by Cournot, emphazises the fact that 'pure competition *results* from certain conditions: this is much better than to posit it as an institutional datum' (Schumpeter 1954: 973). Premises of a theory of *imperfect* competition thus blossomed in the ninetheenth century, relying on the strategic interaction between agents. Cournot-Bertrand oligopoly, as well as Edgeworth's contract curve, portray agents behaving strategically, contrary to the assumption of price-taking behaviour postulated by perfect competition. The latter behaviour only appears as a limit case, corresponding to an infinity of agents.

If Cournot, Bertrand and Edgeworth have paved the way to a rigorous analysis of oligopolistic markets, they are still concerned with economic rivalry about a *homogeneous* product: all sellers are supposed to sell the same product. It was Hotelling (1929) and Chamberlin (1933) who pointed out the consequences of abandoning the third key assumption of a perfectly competitive market, namely, the assumption of perfect homogeneity of the product. In particular, in a superb article devoted to the analysis of spatial competition, Hotelling provides a penetrating analysis of price competition between two sellers where their rivalry grows more intense, the closer they are located to each other. When they are located well apart from each other, they constitute 'local monopolies', but each has less access to the customers of his rival: a decrease in the latter's price has little effect on demand. On the other hand, when sellers get closer to each other, they are more likely to enter a price war, but a small decrease in price may entail a significant increase in demand. It is easy to recognize here the spatial analogue of *product differentiation*: when two products are close substitutes, price competition will be harsher than between products with a weaker degree of substitutability.

Finally, concerning the consequences of consumers' *imperfect information* on the strategies of firms, it is only recently that these have been taken into consideration by economists. Stigler (1961) and Akerlof (1970) were among the first to insist on the importance of imperfect information of economic agents to understand numerous economic market phenomena. But the study of the strategic aspects of imperfect information is still more recent, and is associated with the problem of *asymmetric information*, in the framework of the so-called 'principal-agent' model (Ross 1973), with the theory of signalling (Spence 1974), and with the contributions related to the theory of insurance markets (Rothschild and Stiglitz 1976).

Contrary to the theory of perfect competition which can be viewed as definitely accomplished, the theory of imperfect competition is still in the process of being elaborated. Recently, it has immensely benefited from the parallel development of another scientific discipline: the theory of games. This theory, introduced by von Neumann and Morgenstern (1945), studies at an abstract level interactive decision processes in which decision agents are conscious of the interdependence of their decisions. The problems posed by the study of imperfect competition are naturally transposable in the language of this theory, so that both of them have benefited from considerable 'cross-fertilization'. Oligopoly situations involving a small number of sellers conscious of their mutual rivalry closely resemble the decisional contexts studied in the framework of game theory. Accordingly, one should not be surprised that game theory plays a leading role among the methods used in the analysis of imperfectly competitive markets.

The four assumptions underlying the paradigm of perfect competition constitute the natural departure points of the theories attempting to explain the functioning of markets under imperfect competition : whenever at least one of these assumptions is violated, imperfect competition is present. Each of these forms of imperfection has given rise to a multiplicity of theoretical developments, and the framework of this book is organized around the four corresponding themes: the role of entry and entry barriers in the degree of market competition (Chapter 3), the differentiation of products (Chapter 4) and the information of agents as an instrument of competition (Chapter 5). Chapter 2 is devoted to a brief presentation of the obstacles to competition. Finally, Chapter 6 illustrates the recent attempts to extend to the general equilibrium model, some contributions formulated initially in the framework of partial analysis.

It is not an easy task to present in a simple manner the models which have been used to analyse imperfect competition . The corresponding market situations are often complex, because they involve rational agents behaving strategically. Furthermore, some basic knowledge of microeconomics is needed in order to understand these models, since they are formulated in the usual language of this theory. Nevertheless, we have tried to provide a readable access to this theory, without sacrificing, we hope, too much rigour in the presentation of the arguments. The microeconomic knowledge required to understand this book is concerned with the notions of *costs* (total, average and marginal), of *utility functions*, and of *indifference curves*; most readers of this book will probably share this minimal knowledge. In any case, precise definitions of these concepts can be found in microeconomics textbooks such as Varian (1993).

It would be an exaggeration to claim that the whole field of imperfect competition could be covered in the framework of such a small book. In particular, the reader should not expect to find in the following pages applications of the theory to privileged domains of microeconomics, such as international trade, industrial economics, public economics, or macroeconomics. The introduction of imperfect competition in trade models has been a flourishing area of research during the last two decades; the interested reader is refered to Helpman and Krugman (1986). Similarly, the relations between the theory of imperfect competition and theoretical industrial economics have been subjected to close scrutiny in the well-known textbook by Tirole (1988). Recently also several papers were devoted to the study of strategic interaction between public and private firms in an industry; see, for instance, de Fraja and Delbono (1989) or Grilo (1994). Implications for macroeconomics are studied for instance by Benassy (1991) or d'Aspremont *et al.* (1991).

2

FROM PERFECT TO IMPERFECT COMPETITION

In this chapter, we shall examine successively each of the assumptions defining perfect competition, and the problems arising when these assumptions are relaxed: barriers to entry and collusion (Section 2.1), product differentiation (Section 2.2), and competition with uninformed consumers (Section 2.3). Section 2.4 is of a methodological nature: it introduces briefly the concepts of game theory used in the analysis of imperfect competition .

2.1 Barriers to entry and collusion

2.1.1 *The assumption of an atomistic market*

The definition of competition proposed by economists differs substantially from its usual meaning. Indeed, the word 'competition' generally evokes a struggle in which firms compete with a view to increasing their market share at the expense of their rivals. The extreme form of this notion corresponds to a predatory behaviour through which firms openly pursue elimination of their competitors. By contrast, the notion of competition, as used in economics textbooks, does not share this agressive connotation. On the contrary, firms in textbooks behave extremely gently with respect to their rivals: they simply ignore their existence! The only signals they take into account are prices of their own inputs and outputs, as they are anonymously indicated by markets. Then they adjust mechanically to the most profitable decision, taking all prices as given.

Let us illustrate the above by a very simple example. Two farmers in the Midwest who produce corn are not viewed as rival producers. The reason is simply that there are so many other farmers producing corn that the contribution of these two particular farmers to the total corn supply can be viewed as infinitesimal. Consequently, neither of these two farmers could imagine that production decisions of his neighbour can in any way affect the results of his own activity. In the same manner, no farmer can imagine being able in isolation to influence the price of corn by the choice of his individual supply. As for the demand side, there are so many bakeries that it would be foolish for a particular baker to hope to pay a lower price for flour than that paid by other bakers: all of them have to accept the price as a datum which they cannot exert any influence on.

This situation corresponds more or less to an 'atomistic' or competitive market, at least in the sense used in economics textbooks.

> Consider a seller who provides so insignificant a part of the total market supply of some homogeneous good that if he raised his asking price, his sales would drop to practically zero, or to zero in the extreme case. And

if he witheld all his supply from the market, the effect on market price would be practically undetectable. If he lowered his price, the increased amount demanded would swamp his available supply. For all intents and purposes, the demand curve he sees facing him for his products is virtually a horizontal line at the prevailing market price. A slightly higher price would reduce his sales to zero while a slightly lower price would increase the amount demanded beyond the amount he can supply. In jargon, the elasticity of demand facing him is infinite. A seller facing an infinitely elastic demand is called a price-taker. This is also sometimes described as an atomistic market (Alchian and Allen 1972).

The assumption of an atomistic market has important implications, because it makes it easy to determine the price and quantity exchanged. To illustrate, consider again the market for corn, with farmers as suppliers, and bakers as demanders, of the product. Suppose there are 500 farmers and 1000 bakers. The total cost of production of a quantity q of corn is, for each farmer, defined by $C(q) = \frac{1}{8} + \frac{q^2}{2}$; $\frac{1}{8}$ is the fixed cost and $\frac{q^2}{2}$ is the variable cost, which increases with the volume of corn. Now consider a particular bakery. If it buys a quantity q of corn (flour), assume that it can produce a number $F(q)$ of loaves of bread equal to $q(1 - \frac{q}{2})$: the marginal product of the baker's labour decreases with the quantity of corn used in the production of loaves. Finally, suppose that each loaf is sold at £1 and that the only cost for the baker is the price p to be paid per unit of corn. Let us show that, if we assume the corn market to be atomistic, both the price and the quantity of corn exchanged between farmers and bakers can easily be determined.

First consider a farmer and assume that p is the price of corn. If this farmer decides to produce a quantity q of corn, he realizes a profit $V(q)$ defined by

$$V(q) = pq - C(q) = pq - \frac{q^2}{2} - \frac{1}{8}. \tag{2.1}$$

Notice that, by letting the value of q be independent of the value of p, we assume implicitly that the market is atomistic: the farmer behaves as a price-taker. If the farmer chooses to produce the quantity q which maximizes his profit, he will supply the market with the quantity of corn which solves $V'(q) = 0$, or $q = p$. Aggregating the individual supplies of the 500 farmers, we obtain the *supply function* of corn as

$$S(p) = 500p. \tag{2.2}$$

Now consider a particular baker. If p is the price of corn and if he buys a quantity q of corn, his profit $B(q)$ is given by

$$B(q) = F(q) - pq = q \left(1 - \frac{q}{2}\right) - pq; \tag{2.3}$$

the first term on the right-hand side of (2.3) represents the receipts obtained from the market for loaves at a unit selling price of £1; the second term represents the buying cost of a quantity q of corn at a unit buying price p. Again we assume in this formulation that our baker is a price-taker both on the market for bread and on the market for corn. If the baker chooses to produce the quantity of loaves which maximizes his profit, he will demand on the market for corn the quantity q which solves $B'(q) = 0$, or $q = 1 - p$. Aggregating the individual demands of the 1000 bakers, we obtain the *demand function* of corn as

$$D(p) = 1000(1 - p). \tag{2.4}$$

Finally, *if we assume that the price of corn clears the market*, a condition necessary to avoid rationing of supply or demand, then transactions take place at the price p^* such that $D(p^*) = S(p^*)$, or, using (2.2) and (2.4), $p^* = \frac{2}{3}$. At this *equilibrium price*, each farmer sells a quantity of corn equal to $\frac{2}{3}$ while each of the 1000 bakers buys a quantity equal to $\frac{1}{3}$. Notice that each farmer makes a strictly positive profit at this equilibrium price. Similarly, each baker realizes a positive profit equal to $\frac{1}{18}$ at the same price.

As stated above, the assumption of an atomistic market allows the market solution in terms of price and quantity to be determined easily. Unfortunately, this assumption discards from the analysis any market situation in which some buyers or sellers would take into account the effect of their individual decision on the exchange price, or the effect of the decisions of their competitors. The market price follows simply from the juxtaposition of individual decisions which, due to the assumption of an atomistic market, are taken without any conscious interdependence among the decision-makers. This assumption can be tenable only when there are a large number of buyers and sellers. Then it is difficult for an isolated agent to exert any individual action on the price-fixing mechanism: his individual supply, or demand, only constitutes an infinitesimal part of the total supply or demand, from which the equilibrium price is derived.

But why should there be a large number of buyers and sellers? On the market for a final good, the multiplicity of buyers can often be explained by the fact that demand essentially emanates from consumers, who are numerous. But, on the supply side, there is no a priori reason why there should be a large number of sellers. With a view to justifying the assumption, economists have imagined the following scenario. As long as there exists the possibility of realizing positive profits, new firms will enter into the industry in order to take advantage of this unexploited treasure. The supply of these new firms has to be added to that of the pre-existing firms, increasing thereby total supply and decreasing the resulting equilibrium price. The profits of all firms in the industry will accordingly decrease, but the process of entry will continue as long as the receipts of the existing firms exceed their production costs. Due to the existence of fixed costs, however, at a certain moment, the equilibrium price will not be high enough to further guarantee positive profits to the last entrant. The entry process will then stop since a new entrant would incur a loss. If the number of firms resulting from this entry process is large enough, the assumption of an atomistic market may also be justified on the supply side.

In order to illustrate the above entry scenario, let us return for a moment to the market for corn we considered above. We noticed that each of the 500 farmers realizes a strictly positive profit at the price p^*. Consequently, according to the scenario we have just described, new farmers are wishing to produce corn, so as to share the same opportunity as the other farmers already operating on the market. Suppose, for instance, that 300 further farmers also decide to start the production of corn, under the same cost conditions. The supply function $S(p)$ now becomes $S(p) = 800p$, and the new equilibrium price, after entry, follows from the equality $800p = 1000(1 - p)$, i.e. $p^* = \frac{5}{9}$: entry entails a decrease in price, leading in turn to a decrease in profits. Nonetheless these profits are still positive, so that the entry scenario can continue. It is easy to see that this will remain the case as long as the number of farmers remains below 1000: for any smaller number, the equilibrium price remains larger than the unit cost. But with 1000 farmers, the supply function is equal to $1000p$, and the equality of demand and supply now provides a new equilibrium price p^* equal to $\frac{1}{2}$, so that 500 units of corn are exchanged on the market, entailing a zero profit level for each farmer. The entry of new farmers has completely eroded the profit of them all. At this *long-run equilibrium*, 1000 farmers and 1000 bakers operate on the corn market, and it seems natural to assume that each one of them cannot have any individual influence on the market mechanism. We must, however, remain cautious and not draw hasty conclusions from the elegance of the above reasoning. Indeed, alternative scenarios can also be imagined which do not drive the market price to the competitive outcome.

2.1.2 *Barriers to entry as an obstacle to competition*

In the corn market allegory, the free entry reasoning presupposes the existence of an *armée de réserve* of farmers who can instantaneously take the decision to produce corn on their fields. It is thus necessary that the ownership of land is sufficiently dispersed to guarantee that this assumption holds. History has, however, seen several periods during which land ownership has been the privilege of a powerful few. Even today, the ownership of some resources is still concentrated in the hands of very few operators; this is the case for some mineral waters, rare paintings, old jewellery, and collections of stamps. In such cases, there exists a barrier to entry simply due to the fact that there is no potential candidate. If this is the case, we find ourselves in a situation of *monopoly*. But the existence of a monopoly is not the only reason why market entry can be denied to potential competitors, thereby protecting the profits of the incumbent firms from erosion. Another natural barrier may follow from cost conditions. For instance, if sunk costs are important, entry can be prevented due to the fact that competition after entry may not generate receipts which are sufficient to cover the expenses of the entrant. Indeed, with high fixed costs, the incumbent firm has to reach high levels of output before being able to cover these costs. The same must hold for the potential entrant, so that total output *after entry* can be so large that it entails a dramatic decrease in market price, so dramatic that profits of both firms may become negative. One firm, and only one firm, can survive on the market: this is the case of *natural monopoly*. In this case, the entry scenario imagined by economists in order to reconstitute an atomistic market cannot be effective: the individual supply of each firm at the equilibrium price after entry represents a too substantial portion of the aggregate supply at that price. In the same spirit, the simple fact that a firm sells a higher-quality product than its potential competitors gives that firm an advantage which can prevent the entry of these lower-quality competitors. Later on, we shall return to this possibility.

The existence of entry barriers which we have just evoked follows from the particular conditions in which firms operate: ownership concentration leading to monopoly, cost advantage or product quality advantage leading to natural monopoly. Probably more interesting is the case of *strategic* entry barriers resulting from a deliberate policy of incumbent firms aiming at discouraging potential competitors from entering the market. Consider for instance a market initially occupied by a monopoly, which cannot rely on natural entry barriers to protect its profits from erosion. Then entry is possible and one should expect other firms to try to take advantage of it. Nevertheless, the incumbent monopoly can choose a price which is lower than that which maximizes its short-run profits, thus rendering entry unattractive to potential entrants. This policy undoubtedly compels the firm to set a more competitive price, while allowing it to maintain its monopoly position. We shall come back at length to the topic of strategic barriers in Chapter 3.

Another example of strategic barriers appears in the context of competition by substitute products. When a new product is introduced, the firm can invade the market by selling a wide variety of different variants of this product, with a view to preventing competitors from settling into 'niches' which have not yet been exploited. Thanks to this 'brand proliferation', the firm discourages the entry of potential competitors. A good illustration of this strategy is provided by a chain store opening several branches in a town before competitors can invest in unexploited districts.

In conclusion, one must admit that several obstacles may arise to prevent the development of the entry scenario invented by economists. Some are related to specific circumstances, others to the strategic behaviour of incumbent firms. But there is another way for these firms to avoid profit erosion, namely by means of *collusion*.

2.1.3 *Collusion as an obstacle to competition*

The most natural way for incumbent firms to avoid suffering from their *mutual* competition is to coordinate their policies by substituting a collective constraint for their individual freedom. Collusive agreements may deal with several objects – such as prices, power delegation, production quotas – and appear in several institutional guises – such as syndicates, professional associations, centralized sales bureaux, product standard agreements. All of them have the same purpose: to protect the market's actors from baneful competition.

To illustrate one of the commonest consequences of such collusion, let us come back to the market for corn analysed above. Let us now suppose that the 1000 farmers, conscious that competition can be mutually detrimental, decide to act in unison, and create to that effect a centralized sales bureau. Then it is not unreasonable to assume that the sales bureau knows the demand function $D(p)$, that is to say knows the price p for which the equality $Q = D(p)$ holds, with Q representing the aggregate output of all farmers. Given (2.4), the price p must satisfy the equality $Q = 1000(1 - p)$. Consequently, the price $p(Q)$ at which a quantity Q of corn can be absorbed by the market is given by

$$p(Q) = 1 - \frac{Q}{1000}.$$

Let us assume that the objective function of the sales bureau, which has to choose the aggregate output, involves maximizing the individual profit of each farmer. Then, supposing that aggregate production is equally shared among the 1000 farmers and denoting by q^* the optimal individual production, the cooperative must solve the problem

$$\max_q \left(1 - \frac{1000q}{1000} \right) q - \frac{q^2}{2} - \frac{1}{8}, \tag{2.5}$$

with solution $q^* = \frac{1}{3}$, and corresponding price $p^* = \frac{2}{3}$. The profit obtained by each farmer is now equal to $\frac{1}{24}$ and, accordingly, strictly positive: coordination of the farmers' supply inside the sales bureau has neutralized competition among them. Thanks to collusion, the long-run equilibrium with zero profits is avoided.

This analysis shows that free entry cannot guarantee by itself the competitive solution. It is also necessary for incumbent firms, aware that their mutual competition leads to profit erosion, not to organize collusion among themselves by agreeing on production quotas with a view to raising the selling price. Nevertheless, as we shall see in the next chapter, collusive agreements can be extremely fragile, not only because they are fought by governments, but also because they are inherently unstable. As the above example shows, the collusive agreement (cartel) is advantageous for its members as long as each one of them respects the production quota which is imposed on him by the agreement. Now there is a permanent temptation for the members of the cartel to 'cheat' and secretely break its rules.

To show this, let us come back again to the above example. The profit of a cartel member is given by (2.5). Examining this expression carefully, we notice that the price $p(q) = 1 - \frac{1000q}{1000}$ would scarcely decrease if a member of the cartel were to increase his supply slightly beyond the quota of $\frac{1}{3}$ imposed by the cartel: total supply remains practically unchanged. Suppose, then, that a member chooses secretely to produce $\frac{2}{3}$ instead of $\frac{1}{3}$. His new profit will then be approximately equal to $p^* \cdot \frac{2}{3} - \frac{4}{18} - \frac{1}{8} = \frac{7}{72}$, which represents a substantial increase in profit, compared with the level of profit the cheating member obtains when respecting the quota ($\frac{3}{72}$). One must accordingly recognize the existence of a permanent temptation, for each farmer, secretely to increase his production, once the cartel agreement has been signed. If several farmers, individually speculating on the faithfulness of the others, start to 'cheat', it might entail a substantial decrease in the selling price and drive the whole cartel to ruin. Thus, there are countervailing forces against collusion, making it vulnerable when it is not explicitly confirmed by a written agreement, open to legal enforcement. But such contracts are generally forbidden by law.

To conclude, the theory built on the assumption of an atomistic market is valid only when the number of market operators is sufficiently large. In order to make this assumption feasible, economists have postulated the free entry of competitors into the market as long as the possibility of making positive profits is not fully exhausted. Then entry increases total supply at each price and, accordingly, leads to a decrease in the competitive price and in the profits of all firms. However, firms have several ways of fighting against profit erosion. First, they can build strategic entry barriers by quoting a price which makes entry unprofitable to any potential entrant. Furthermore, they can coordinate their supply policies with a view to keeping the market price sufficiently high. Finally there are situations – monopolies or natural monopolies – in which entry is impossible by virtue of the very conditions in which firms have to operate. All these situations correspond to circumstances which are at the heart of theories of imperfect competition, and which will be analysed in the forthcoming chapters.

2.2 Product differentiation

2.2.1 *The assumption of a homogeneous product*

The presence of a large number of buyers and sellers is the first requirement for a competitive market. But it is not the only one. We also assume that the units of the good exchanged in the market are viewed as identical by all participants. To understand the meaning of this assumption, it is useful to go back to the neoclassical theory of consumer behaviour (see, for instance, Varian 1993: Chapter 4). Consumer choice operates among commodity bundles, which are ranked according to preference ordering. When two commodity bundles are viewed as equivalent in terms of these preferences, they belong to the same indifference class, or to the same indifference curve in the case of two goods. Two products A and B are defined as *homogeneous* or *perfect substitutes* if, for all consumers of these products, indifference curves are lines with unit negative slope.

In Fig. 2.1, all points on the solid line share the property that the sum of their coordinates is equal to one. Furthermore, all of them are on the same indifference curve which coincides with the line: if the consumer must choose between the commodity bundles (a, b) and (a', b'), he is indifferent between them. This means that, when equal quantities of product A are substituted for product B, or vice versa, consumers' preferences are not modified: product A is a perfect substitute for product B. This property has an important implication in terms of the purchase behaviour of the consumer, when faced with different prices for

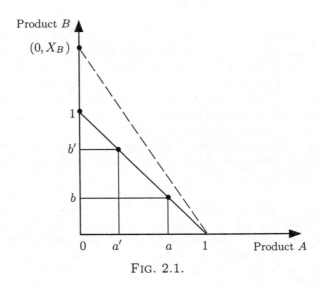

$$\text{FIG. 2.1.}$$

products A and B. Suppose for instance that the price P_A of product A is equal to one and higher than the price P_B of product B.

Then the budgetary constraint of the consumer, when he owns one unit of income, which requires that $P_A X_A + P_B X_B = 1$, is represented on the same figure by a line whose slope is less than -1 and goes through the point $(0, 1)$ (the dashed line in Fig. 2.1). The preferred point on this line is clearly the point $(0, X_B)$: the consumer then buys only product B. In the opposite case, when $P_A < P_B$, it is easy to see that the consumer buys only product A. Consequently, when two firms supply the market with products which are perfect substitutes, all consumers choose to buy the product from the firm quoting the lowest price, however small the price differential. It is easy to see that it is then that competition will be fiercest. On the other hand, when the two products are not perfect substitutes, and when price P_A is different from P_B, nothing will prevent some consumers persisting in buying the most expensive one: this will be the case, for instance, when $P_A > P_B$, but some consumers consider that variant A is of a higher quality than variant B. The firm selling product B should then lower further its price if it wants to convince these consumers that the advantage realized on the price differential compensates for the loss incurred in passing from the quality of product A to that of product B. Thus, it follows that if a firm wants to escape to unavoidable competition when a homogeneous product is sold, it has to supply the market with a product which is not a perfect substitute for those existing already in the industry. Doubtless, it will still be subject to competition from the other firms, to the extent that they sell substitutes for its product. But the homogeneity assumption is no longer satisfied, and we enter the domain of imperfect competition. In conclusion, we define two products as being differentiated when consumers base their purchase decisions not only on price differences, but also on certain intrinsic characteristics of each, which are not shared in the same proportions by the other.

2.2.2 *How to differentiate one's product*

There are several ways through which firms can succeed in differentiating their products from those supplied by their competitors. Even when a firm sells a product which is identical to that sold by its rivals, it can choose to sell it at a different location, in which case it is subject to less severe competition. The reason is that consumers who are located closer to this firm than to its competitors prefer to buy the product, at an equal price, from it than from its rivals. This is so because it allows these consumers to save on all forms of transportation costs they would otherwise incur, such as petrol and time. An appropriate choice of selling point creates a kind of 'local monopoly' with respect to consumers located close to this point, to the extent that farther competitors should consent sufficient discounts in view of covering the costs of their moving. For example, consider two grocery stores, A and B, selling the same products but located in a town at some distance from each other. If they sell their product at exactly the same price, those located closer to A buy from A, while those closer to B buy from B. By decreasing its price, B can attract some fraction of the customers of A, but the decrease will have to be substantial if the distance between the shops is large, and if B wants to attract all of them. The products sold by A and B are then strongly differentiated. On the other hand, when the two grocery stores are very close to each other, a very small price differential will be sufficient to capture all the customers of the rival firm. Then product differentiation is only weak. The extreme case where both grocery stores are located next to each other corresponds to the situation of perfectly homogeneous products, considered in the context of perfect competition.

A firm can also differentiate its product from that of its competitors by supplying its customers with a quality of service which is more or less satisfactory. Scherer (1979) gives as an example the case of two supermarkets supplying more or less the same goods. In one of them, the employees are well trained and polite; the stores are attractive and beautifully decorated. The other one has a shortage of employees, entailing bottlenecks in front of the cashiers; products are also presented in a rudimentary manner, without any particular effort. Most probably this negative aspect will be compensated by the fact that prices are lower here than there. This does not prevent some consumers persisting in buying from the dearer shop, simply because they pay more attention to the quality of the service, which compensates for the higher prices.

On the other hand, product differentiation may simply follow from the intrinsic characteristics of the products, which change from one variant to the other: shirts can be synthetic or linen, and TV sets can be black and white or colour. Some cars can be sportscars, while others are family cars. The first two examples correspond to cases of *vertical* product differentiation, while the latter to *horizontal* differentiation. Under vertical differentiation, all consumers buy the same variant when both are sold at the same price. Under horizontal differentiation, some consumers prefer to buy one variant and some the other, when they are sold at the same price.

Finally, product differentiation can be entirely, or partially, subjective when it is exclusively, or mainly, created by the subjective perception of the consumer's imagination. Some cigarettes differ from others only by the type of advertising through which they are promoted, and some products, though perfectly identical to others in terms of their intrinsic characteristics, are more easily sold simply because their packaging is more attractive. Firms spend huge amounts of money on creating an 'image' through which consumers identify their product, and accordingly resist to the temptation of buying the rivals' variants. This struggle, which can become exacerbated in the case of comparative advertising, reveals of course that the industry in which it happens is far from being competitive.

2.2.3   *Demand structure and product differentiation*

Following Lancaster (1966), a product is considered to be defined as a bundle of services provided to the consumer. For instance, a car allows its owner to move around according to his needs. This motion arises in particular conditions of comfort and security which vary with the type of car considered. Furthermore, beyond its purely utilitarian aspects, the car also allows its owner to portray an image of his position on the social scale, as reflected by the brand, the power, or the particular design of the car, all elements which influence the purchase decision of the consumer. This definition of a product, which relies on the services provided, called *characteristics* or *attributes*, allows a precise definition of differentiated products. These are products which have the same characteristics, but they have them in different proportions. Accordingly, when faced with a purchase decision, consumers consider not only price differences, but also differences among the levels of characteristics existing between the variants supplied by firms.

With products defined as bundles of characteristics existing in certain proportions, it starts to be easy to formulate the preferences of consumers among varieties also in terms of their characteristics. More precisely, it is generally assumed that a consumer can be identified with a particular bundle of attributes, corresponding to the 'ideal' variant in terms of his preferences. The diversity of tastes among consumers is then translated into the language of the theory by assuming that consumers differ according to their ideal products. Thus, in one of the examples considered above, while the sportscar is the ideal product for a young sportsman, the ideal car for a father of four would most probably be the family model. In practice, not all ideal products can be supplied on the market, due to the existence of fixed costs of production related to each particular variant. Then consumers have to resort to products which are more or less remote from their ideal variant. The farther a product is from the ideal variant, the higher the loss of satisfaction of the consumer. In several cases (and in particular for durable goods), the consumer buys only one variant, to the exclusion of others.

Given his willingness to pay, he will choose to buy the variant giving him the highest surplus, taking into account both of how far away variants supplied are from his ideal product, and of the prices at which these products are supplied.

The total demand addressed to a particular firm then follows from aggregation of individual purchase decisions, as they have just been described. This demand clearly depends both on the price and on the levels of characteristics of the variant chosen by the firm. But it also depends on the prices and the levels of characteristics of all substitute products supplied by competitors. This interdependence among demands addressed to the various firms is at the very origin of the strategic interaction among them. In the case of differentiated products, this interaction takes a particular form: the closer the products of the firms in terms of the level of their attributes, the fiercer the competition among them. More precisely, each variant is in direct competition with its 'neighbours' in the space of characteristics. When a particular firm increases its sales of a product, due to a price decrease, this is only detrimental to firms which sell the closest variants to it. Then competition is said to be *localized*. For instance, in the case of the car market, some models (such as the VW Golf and the Ford Escort) are in direct competition while others (such as the Lada Riva and the Rolls-Royce Silver Spur) are not. The result of this particular form of competition is market segmentation, a segment being defined as the set of consumers who buy a particular variant. The interaction between two products which are not neighbours in the space of characteristics takes a different form: it goes along a chain of products which are, pair-wise, direct competitors. We have just said that the increase in sales of a particular product has no direct impact in case of localized competition on the sales of products which are not directly comparable. Nevertheless, it must be expected that those firms which are concerned by the increase in demand for this product will react by adjusting their own price. This will affect in turn the demand for the neighbours of these products, and so on, entailing a chain of reactions which could finally affect all firms operating in the industry.

We can illustrate the above in the following way. Consider a circular boulevard, as in Fig. 2.2, on each point of which is located a consumer who is willing to buy a unit of some product. Four shops selling this product are located, respectively, at the points A, B, C and D on the boulevard. If all shops sell a unit of the product at the same price, each shop obtains a quarter of the market, constituted by all consumers who are closer to it than to the other shops (for instance, the segment (a_1, a_2) on Fig. 2.2 for the shop located in A). If shop A slightly decreases its price, it will gain the sets of consumers located in the segments (a'_1, a_1) and (a'_2, a_2). Shops B and D experience a fall in demand, but not C. Now suppose (see Fig. 2.2) that the consumers located along the boulevard have to go through the centre O to reach any of the four shops. In this case the distance to any shop is the same and equal to twice the radius of the circle. Consequently, if one of the shops decreases its price from a situation where each of them quotes the same price, all consumers will not be willing to buy from

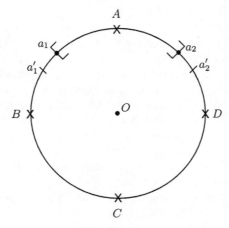

FIG. 2.2.

this shop, whereas they would have bought indifferently from any of them before the price decrease. In this case, competition is delocalized and the chain effect described above no longer exists. Everything is as if shops sold a perfectly homogeneous product, and only price differences, and not location, play a role in consumers' choice to buy from a particular firm.

2.2.4 *Product differentiation, market structure and entry*

In its purest formulation, the competitive assumption considers that firms entering the market sell the same homogeneous product as incumbent firms. Assuming further that consumers are perfectly informed, competition among firms does not allow any price differential for, otherwise, all consumers would buy from the firm quoting the lowest price. Consequently, the increase in supply due to entry uniformly affects the profits of all firms operating in the industry. On the other hand, when entry in the industry takes place with firms selling differentiated products, nothing can prevent these firms from obtaining a positive market share even if they do not set the same price as quoted by firms already in the market. Furthermore, at least in the case of 'localized' competition, the effects of entry are no longer the same for all firms. These effects proceed along a chain of interactions between 'neighbouring' firms, and become weaker and weaker in proportion as these firms sell products which are farther away from the new product introduced by the entrant. In this case, industry structure and effects of entry are more difficult to identify. In particular, the question is raised as to where the industry begins and where it ends.

To illustrate, let us come back to the spatial analogy of product differentiation which was proposed above. Consider a road along which are located five villages A, B, C, E and F, say. Each village is located at a distance equal to d from its immediate neighbour, except villages C and E which are separated by a distance equal to $2d$ (see Fig. 2.3). Furthermore, a bakery is located in each

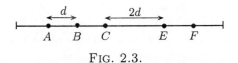

Fig. 2.3.

village, producing loaves at the same unit cost c. Every day, the inhabitants of each village consume exactly one loaf, from which they obtain a utility level equal to s. When they decide to buy their bread in a neighbouring village, they incur a transportation cost equal to the distance d. We suppose that $c + d < c + 2d$. This assumption guarantees that, if any bakery in the group of villages (A, B, C) sold its bread at a price equal to unit cost, it would succeed in attracting the customers located in an adjacent village, without incuring losses ($c + d < s$); but it would be unable to do it for more distant villages. In particular, the bakery in C cannot attract the customers located in E without incuring losses, since their reservation price s is smaller than their total cost $c + 2d$. In the same manner, bakeries in the group (E, F) can attract the inhabitants located in the village of their rival in the group, but they cannot attract without incurring a loss those located in village C and, a fortiori, those in A and B.

This example illustrates both the 'chain structure' of demand in the case of differentiated products, and the interdependence of firms' demands, which generates strategic interaction among them. There are in fact *two* industries in the above example: the first constituted by the group of firms (A, B, C) and the other by the group (E, F). On the other hand, there is no interdependence between demands of firms in the first group and in the second.

Now, in the same example, suppose that a new bakery is opened at point D, midway between villages C and E. Then this bakery becomes a direct potential competitor of both bakeries located in C and E, since it can attract their customers by selling its bread at unit cost (remember that $c + d < s$). The two industries (A, B, C) and (E, F), which were initially separated, are now brought together due to the entry of firm D. Accordingly, the entry of this single firm has considerably reinforced competition, to the extent that the industry structure moves from a situation consisting of two groups of firms with a small number of firms in each, to a new situation consisting of a single industry with six firms, the demands of which are all interrelated.

By way of conclusion, it appears that entry with differentiated products has much more subtle implications than when entry is realized with a homogeneous product. First, the potential entrant now has the faculty of supplying a product which is particularly designed to meet the needs of customers. To that effect, he will choose a product optimally 'localized' in the space of characteristics, given the different 'ideal' variants of the consumers and given the existing products already supplied by the incumbent firms. He can also, in some cases, supply several variants of the same product, so as to occupy a larger number of 'niches' which otherwise would be occupied later by rival firms. In all these cases, product and price selection have strategic aspects which are not compatible with the competitive assumption.

On the other hand, it should be expected that entry barriers related to sunk or production costs are more frequently observed when entry takes place with differentiated products. Furthermore, the size of the market corresponding to a particular variant inside a range of substitute products is rather small, preventing a full use of scale economies. For instance, the 'density' of retail shops in a particular city is limited, because the market is too 'narrow' to allow the sunk costs of a new entrant to be covered when a given number of shops are already established in the city. Such entry barriers, related to sunk costs and to the size of the market, lead necessarily to a small number of competing firms and, accordingly, to an oligopolistic market structure.

Finally, entry barriers related to quality differences can be observed when competition bears on the *quality* of the products (vertical product differentiation), allowing the survival of a small number of firms only. The existence of such barriers is particularly likely when the diversity of consumers is weak, in terms of their tastes and/or income levels. In that case, firms which supply the market with products of higher quality can prevent the entry of firms wishing to supply more standardized variants: even quoting much lower prices does not allow a positive market share to be captured. On the other hand, a more dispersed income distribution, for instance, could lead to a wider range of products coexisting on the market, with luxurious and standardized variants simultaneously present, and generating more effective competition among firms.

To conclude, then, given the above considerations – chain demands, the possibility of selecting the variant of the product, the existence of entry barriers related to cost structures or quality differentials – one must expect a smaller number of competing firms in a differentiated industry than in an industry selling a homogeneous product. Furhermore, due to the interdependence of the demand functions of the firms, they should be expected to take into consideration the strategic aspects of their interaction. These are natural ingredients of imperfect competition, and it is easy to understand why the supporters of the perfectly competitive paradigm have introduced the assumption of a homogeneous product.

2.3 Imperfect information as an obstacle to competition

2.3.1 *The assumption of perfect information*

Beyond assumptions concerning the number of agents and product homogeneity, perfect competition also requires that both sellers and buyers have perfect information concerning the price and the quality of the product exchanged on the market .

The problem of perfect information about prices at which goods and services are exchanged is one of the most debatable questions of economic theory. It cannot be answered, indeed, without having answered the question of how prices are formed. A particular aspect of this question is who quotes the prices. Two alternative theories have been proposed by economists to answer this question.

The first theory assumes that the power of fixing prices is devolved to an 'auctioneer' who coordinates the decisions of the agents with a view to reducing in each market the discrepancy between the quantity supplied and the quantity demanded of the corresponding good. In order to achieve this, the auctioneer is assumed to decrease the price whenever the supply of a good exceeds its demand, and to increase when the reverse occurs. Transactions are supposed to take place only when excess supply (or demand) is zero on every market (Walrasian tâtonnement process).

The second theory rests on the idea that firms directly compete on price: then the sellers themselves are assumed to be price-setters. What is the expected result of such a direct competition? If the product is homogeneous, and if all sellers do not quote the same price, perfect knowledge of the distribution of announced selling prices implies that all potential buyers would want to buy from the seller quoting the lowest price. Accordingly, the other sellers will have to lower their own price in order to retain customers. Nevertheless, as long as the joint price exceeds the unit production cost, it is always possible to undercut, thereby increase one's market share and compensate by the increase in sales for the loss due to price reduction. The process of undercutting can only stop when a further price decrease generates a smaller receipt than the cost incurred to satisfy the marginal increase in sales: according to this theory, the resulting price must necessarily be equal to marginal cost.

Thanks to the possibilities opened by arbitrage, this theory can even remain valid when not all potential buyers have full information on price distribution, but only a subset of them. Suppose, indeed, that firms do not quote the same price, but that some agents are aware of the existing price differences. These informed agents will want to buy the product at its lowest price, and resell it at a higher price, thereby increasing the demand for the low-priced firm and increasing the supply of the high-priced one. This in turn will entail that both prices should necessarily converge to a unique value.

The first of the above theories does not tell a very credible story: most markets do not have an auctioneer, and firms themselves decide about their own prices. As for the second theory, it rests crucially on the assumption of perfect information: without it, it is impossible to explain the uniqueness of the selling price and its decrease to the marginal cost of production. No doubt, the possibilities opened by arbitrage weaken somewhat the assumption of perfect knowledge of the price distribution. But still, transaction costs related to arbitrage can be important, and cancel its potential advantage.

Exactly as the assumption of perfect information on prices guarantees that no firm can sell at a price which exceeds the market price, the assumption of perfect information about the *quality* of the products implies that firms must supply a product which is congruent with the quality level supplied by the other firms. If a firm were to 'cheat', and sell a variant of lower quality than the 'market standard', it would be immediately identified and abandoned by customers who would prefer to buy from firms selling a product which is congruent with this market standard. Competition then prevents firms from cheating as to the quality of their products.

It is a commonplace observation that different units of the same product are often sold at different prices in different locations. It is also a commonplace observation that several firms cheat on the quality of their products (products which are more or less fresh, or more or less safe). These observations cannot be explained without the presence of imperfect information about the price distribution or about the characteristics of the products. There are multiple reasons why imperfect information should be frequently observed. Prices are often subjected to shocks caused by inventory conditions, business cycles, demand fluctuations or strategic behaviour of firms. Consumers are used to a noisy environment in which it is difficult to identify the 'market price' at any moment, and thus the discrepancy between this price and the price of a particular firm. On the other hand, the consumer cannot obtain perfect information without previously examining the whole distribution of prices proposed by the various sellers. The geographic dispersion of these sellers often requires a search process which generates important search costs for the potential buyer. He may prefer to satisfy himself with a limited amount of information which he obtains at the closer shops, rather than proceed to a costly exhaustive search.

As for the firms, which are conscious of the existence of these costs, they can lower their selling price in order to reduce consumers' incentives to look for still lower prices. Even better: they can propose to refund their customers the difference in the price, should these customers find a lower price elsewhere. Being now convinced of the 'honesty' of the firm, consumers do not search further, and accordingly allow this firm to set with impunity a higher price than its competitor! These two examples show that to manipulate the information of potential buyers can be a voluntary strategic objective for the firm, as soon as the search for information generates a cost to consumers.

2.3.2 *The consequences of imperfect information*

The existence of imperfect information entails several consequences. First, imperfect information of consumers about prices allows firms to exert market power. Since it is costly to search for information, consumers are tempted to avoid such costs and prefer inertia: they are satisfied with the information they already have, and do not actively look for the lowest price. Firms are aware of this tendency, and some of them can accordingly quote prices which exceed the unit cost of production without creating incentives for further search. Rival firms may eventually react and lower their own price. But why should they do so since, in any case, search costs are so high that consumers do not search and, accordingly, remain unaware of the price decrease? Of course they can themselves inform consumers about their decision to lower their price, but this also generates a cost. It may be unclear whether the benefit expected from informing customers will compensate for this information cost which has to be borne by firms. In this case, the natural competitive mechanism which decreases the market price to the level of the marginal cost of production is no longer operating, and all firms in the industry may obtain substantial profits by quoting prices well above the unit cost of production.

On the other hand, when consumers are imperfectly informed and search is costly, the entry of new firms can entail perverse effects. If there are a large number of firms in the industry, and if one of them lowers its price, only a small number of consumers will be aware of the price decrease. Again, the firms know this and, accordingly, do not feel naturally inclined to use a policy generating such a small increase in profits. By contrast, if the industry is an oligopoly, consumers can only buy from a restricted number of rival firms, so that if one of them lowers its price, it can provoke a more active search among consumers, thereby reinforcing the competitive effects of rivalry pricing. This analysis suggests that, under imperfect information, competition can be harsher under oligopoly than with a large number of firms.

Furthermore, when information is imperfect, the same product can be sold at different prices by different firms, even if it is perfectly homogeneous. A firm can quote a relatively low price because it expects to attract a large number of consumers with rather low search costs, while another firm specializes in a smaller number of consumers with higher search costs who are willing to accept a higher price. The information barrier indeed prevents these customers from being aware of the existence of lower prices.

Finally, firms themselves can let their price fluctuate, sometimes charging a lower, and sometimes a higher, price. This strategy aims at creating noise which perturbs the flow of information channelled to the consumers. It weakens the competition which would otherwise spontaneously develop among them, to the extent that a collective policy of stable prices conveys more and more information on price differentials.

Now, consider the consequences of imperfect information of consumers about the *quality* of the products. Generally, production costs diminish when the quality of the product decreases. Accordingly, it must be expected that firms will take advantage of the imperfect information of consumers, and systematically propose for sale lower-quality products than those which they would have to sell if consumers could identify without any ambiguity the intrinsic characteristics of the products. There exists, however, an automatic punishment against a firm which permanently supplied a variant of lower quality than the average supplied by other firms: it would lose simultaneously its reputation and its customers! But the search for quality is costly, as is the search for a lower price. The resulting consumers' inertia can be as well exploited by firms when selecting the quality of their products. It can be in their interest to select a quality which is inferior to the quality they would have spontaneously supplied if consumers had full information on the characteristics of the existing products. Doubtless, rival firms could provide unsatisfied customers with higher-quality variants, in spite of their higher costs. But, again, these customers should be aware of this increase in quality, and the information barrier can prevent this condition from occurring: the reputation effect cannot play fully its punishment role, except perhaps in the very long run. It is true also that firms selling higher-quality products can inform consumers of the existing quality differential, bearing themselves the cost generated by this information transmission. But more than cost, it is the incredulity of the consumers which could convince firms that they should not use this policy. These consumers are, indeed, submerged under a permanent flow of contradictory advertising messages, and it is difficult for them to separate truth from lies. Often this incredulity is well founded, for the reputation of a firm is frequently based on information received by word of mouth and rumour, which can easily misinterpret reality. When the reputation of a firm is not established on the intrinsic quality of its product, but on a rumour generating more or less erroneous beliefs in consumers, this firm can charge a higher price than its competitors, even if these competitors sell higher-quality variants! Nevertheless, such a situation cannot last for ever since false reputations always end up being exposed. But the transitory period needed to establish truth can be very long and entail significant welfare losses.

In order to fight this natural distrust on the part of its consumers, a firm selling a better variant can offer with its product a system of *warranty* stating that it promises to replace the product should it fail. This system undeniably plays the role of a positive signal for consumers concerning the quality of the product. But its effect is rather limited. The firm may, indeed, fear the consumer himself provoking the failure, since he is in any case covered against the risk by the warranty. Furthermore, it is often very costly to make the warranty operational, for the conditions of its use can be so ambiguous or so restrictive that it would be a nightmare to complain.

Finally, the variety of products supplied in the industry can also be affected by the existence of imperfect information. In a perfectly competitive environment, a variant would be automatically produced and sold whenever its price exceeded its unit cost. With imperfect information, search costs of consumers can prevent the appearance of some variants: consumers who know of its existence would be too few to generate positive profits. Then it must be expected that the range of variants would be narrower than in a world of perfect information, thus creating a more oligopolistic market structure than otherwise.

On the other hand, when two firms sell products intrinsically different but undistinguishable by uninformed consumers, the price war between them will be more severe than it would have been if consumers had been aware of the quality differential. As a consequence of this price war, perhaps only the high-quality variant could have survived under perfect information: the existence of the low-quality variant is only due to imperfect information. In this case, the range of existing variants will be broader than would have been observed if consumers had shared full information on product quality.

The above analysis reveals that imperfect information makes much more difficult the understanding of competition in an industry. Firms can use specific strategies relying on the interaction of their own decisions with those of their rivals. This is the domain of imperfect competition, and these questions should accordingly be considered in the present framework. They will be analysed in greater detail in Chapter 5. But we must first introduce a method of analysis allowing us to take into account the decision context of imperfect competition, namely, situations involving a small number of decision-makers who are conscious of their strategic interaction. The assumptions of perfect competition discard from the analysis precisely market situations of this type, since the price-taking behaviour guarantees that agents neglect their own potential influence on their payoffs, as well as the influence of their rivals in the industry. On the other hand, when competition is imperfect, strategic interaction is explicitly recognized by the agents themselves, or at least by some of them. What then is, the 'market equilibrium' which should be expected? The next section tries to answer this question.

2.4 Imperfect competition and game theory

2.4.1 *Cooperation versus non-cooperation*

Consider the following game in which two players can choose between two strategies: either to put £10 into a box, or to put nothing. Each player makes his choice in ignorance of the strategy chosen by his opponent. After they have made their decision, a referee observes the amount which is in the box, adds to this amount a further 50%, and divides the result between the two players. For example, if each player has chosen to put £10 in the box, the referee adds £10 himself, and each player receives £15.

The payoffs of this game can be summarized in a matrix whose entries consist of the gains (losses) to the players corresponding to the strategies they have selected. For instance, the entry −2.5/7.5 corresponds to the situation where the first player has selected the £10 strategy and the second the £0.

Player 1 \ Player 2	£10	£0
£10	5 / 5	−2.5 / 7.5
£0	7.5 / −2.5	0 / 0

First, notice that if each player could observe the strategy selected by his opponent and communicate with him, both of them would certainly choose the £10 strategy; otherwise, if a player sees his opponent select the £0 strategy he will certainly choose the same strategy himself. If both agree to select the £10 strategy – and who wouldn't – each of them gains £5. Now, which outcome should be expected when each player chooses his strategy in ignorance of the strategy chosen by his opponent? Simple reasoning leads to the conclusion that the only reasonable selection for each player is to play the £0. By way of explanation, consider player 1. He thinks as follows: 'If player 2 has chosen to put £10 in the box, what is the best strategy for me? If I choose the same strategy, my gain is equal to £5; if I choose to put in nothing, my gain is £7.5. Consequently, in this case, the best strategic selection is certainly to put in nothing. Now, suppose that my opponent has chosen the £0 strategy. If I do the same, I lose nothing. But if I put in £10, I lose £2.5. Thus, in this case also, the optimal strategy is to put in nothing. Accordingly, whatever the strategy chosen by the opponent, the best option for player 1 is the £0 strategy. The same reasoning logically applies to player 2 when faced with the same conjectures about the strategic choice of player 1, so that he should be led to an identical conclusion: the best strategy is £0. Furthermore, each player should think that his opponent can reason in the same way as himself, which can only reinforce the conviction that the £0 strategy is indeed the optimal choice. Notice that the above game corresponds to a typical situation where players are conscious of the interactive context of their decision-making: player 1 knows that his payoff depends on the strategic choice of player 2, and vice versa.

Now consider the following example consisting of a market with two sellers of a homogeneous product. Both of them are aware that the higher the selling price, the lower the total quantity sold. To simplify, assume that each of them is allowed to sell either 400 units of the product, or 100 units. Furthermore, the unit price is £100 when 800 units are sold, £200 when 500 units are sold, and £500 when 200 units are sold: the unit price increases in proportion as total quantity decreases. Each seller can choose between two strategies: 400 or 100. The corresponding profits, according to the pair of strategies they have chosen, are identified in the following chart:

Firm 1 \ Firm 2	400	100
400	40 000 / 40 000	80 000 / 20 000
100	20 000 / 80 000	50 000 / 50 000

Again we recognize in this chart the interaction between the decisions of the two sellers, since the profits of each of them depend not only on his own decision, but also on the strategy selected by his opponent. If sellers were allowed to coordinate their choice of strategies and wished to do so, they would certainly elect to sell each 100 units of the product and realize profits of £50 000. Any alternative selection would be rejected by at least one seller. To show this consider for instance the pair (400,100). It is clear that the second seller would not accept this arrangement since, knowing that firm 1 sells 400 units, it would be better for him also to supply 400 units and to make £40 000 profit, which exceeds the £20 000 profit realized at the pair (400,100). Similarly, it would be unreasonable to coordinate their choice on the pair (400,400): then they would each obtain £40 000, while at the pair (100,100) each of them gets £50 000!

Now assume that, for any reason whatsoever, the sellers are not allowed to coordinate their individual decisions when selecting which quantity to send to the market. What are the expected strategic choices now? The answer to this question is really crucial because, if a simple argument can allow us to identify which strategies are selected, the same argument could then be extended later to all market situations in which payoffs to the operators do not depend on their own decision alone, but also on the decision made by their rivals, a typical context in imperfect competition . To provide the beginnings of an answer, let us come back to the situation of two sellers which we have just considered. First, one should not expect a pair of strategies in which one of the sellers – seller 1, say – sells 400 units while the other (seller 2) sells 100 units. It is clear, indeed, that in this situation, seller 2, correctly anticipating the choice of his competitor, would rather sell 400 units as well, and realize a profit of £40 000 (instead of £20 000): such a deviation increases his profit. It would be unreasonable to describe as 'equilibrium' a situation in which one of the sellers could increase his profit by deviating unilaterally from this situation. Is it more reasonable to view the pair of strategies (100,100) as an 'equilibrium'? Clearly not, since each seller in this situation would increase his payoff by selecting the alternative strategy 400: his gain is now £80 000 instead of £50 000. By contrast, if both competitors choose to sell each 400 units, it is easy to verify that no profitable unilateral deviation from this pair of strategies can be identified. This pair is thus characterized by an 'equilibrium' property, to the extent that no seller is willing to deviate from it unilaterally: such a result is called a *non-cooperative equilibrium*.

The major argument underlying the concept of non-cooperative equbrium is that it would be unreasonable to qualify as 'equilibrium' a pair of strategies at which one of the players could benefit from a unilateral move out of this pair, taking into acccount the strategy selected by his opponent: the very existence of this incentive to move makes the corresponding result not credible as an equilibrium position. On the other hand, any pair of strategies at which any unilateral deviation is unprofitable appears as an equilibrium. This equilibrium is non-cooperative because it does not require any coordination between the players to become effective. By contrast, when coordination is possible, the players want to select a pair of strategies such that there exists no other pair of strategies where the payoffs of *both* players can simultaneously increase: any pair of strategies satisfying this criterion is called a *cooperative equilibrium* (the pair of strategies (£10,£10) in the first game considered above, or the pair (100,100) in the second one).

The concepts just presented belong to game theory, a discipline concerned precisely with interactive decision processes. For this theory, a game consists of the specification of a list of n *players* $i, i = 1, \ldots, n$, and, for each one of them, of a set of *strategies* S_i and a *payoff function* $P_i(s_1, \ldots, s_i, \ldots, s_n)$ giving the payoff to player i corresponding to the n-tuple of strategies $(s_1, \ldots, s_i, \ldots, s_n)$. In its abstract language, game theory then proposes the two following equilibrium concepts. An n-tuple $(s'_1, \ldots, s'_i, \ldots, s'_n)$, $s'_i \in S_i$, is a *cooperative equilibrium* if there exists no other n-tuple $(s_1, \ldots, s_n)$, $s_i \in S_i$, such that, for all i, $P_i(s_1, \ldots, s_n) > P_i(s'_1, \ldots, s'_n)$. An n-tuple $(s^*_1, \ldots, s^*_i, \ldots, s^*_n)$ of strategies is a *non-cooperative equilibrium* if, for each player i,

$$P_i(s^*_1, \ldots, s_i, \ldots, s^*_n) \leq P_i(s^*_1, \ldots, s^*_i, \ldots, s^*_n)$$

for all $s_i \in S_i$. We recognize in this abstract language the definitions introduced for the two particular games we have considered above. In both cases, the cooperative equilibria shared the property that no *simultaneous* deviation of the two players from the corresponding equilibrium could increase the payoff of each player. In the same manner, no *unilateral* deviation of a player from a non-cooperative equilibrium can increase his payoff .

Given the above comments, it is not surprising that game theory and economic theory (in particular the theory of imperfect competition) have both benefited from cross-fertilization during the last two decades. Game theory has proposed to economists a theoretical framework in which they can rigorously formulate the problems which are met in the economic analysis of markets. Conversely, this analysis constitutes a privileged field of application for game theory which could otherwise appear as exaggerately abstract. In the following we shall repeatedly use the concepts of equilibria just defined. It is easy to guess how many situations evoked above in this chapter could naturally be formulated by means of these concepts. For instance, when a small number of sellers are conscious of the interactive strategic context created by their simultaneous selection of product supply, this selection can be viewed as a non-cooperative equilibrium when sellers do not coordinate their choices, and as a cooperative equilibrium when they enter into collusion to select their aggregate supply and share the production of it among themselves. Before closing this chapter, we still must briefly review the various *market structures* which have interested economists and which constitute the canvas of a theory of imperfect competition.

2.4.2 *Market structures*

The following chart provides a general picture of the various market structures analysed in imperfect competition. Here these structures are defined by reference to the 'degree of competition' observed on the 'selling side' of the market.

	One seller	Few sellers	Many sellers
Homogeneous product	Homogeneous monopoly	Homogeneous oligopoly	Perfect competition
Differentiated product	Differentiated monopoly	Differentiated oligopoly	Monopolistic competition

For instance, for the case of 'homogeneous monopoly', we assume that the selling side of the market is represented by a single agent (who can be a monopolist or a consortium of all sellers of a good). By contrast, the buying side of the market is assumed to be composed of a large number of potential buyers behaving as price-takers (as in the case of bakers considered above). The same assumption will be made throughout in what follows for all market structures considered. The definitions for competition on the buying side are 'symmetric' (for instance, the market is said to be perfectly competitive on the buying side when buyers are so numerous that their individual fraction of total demand is infinitesimal and cannot affect the price when modified). When this property is not satisfied, the door is opened to strategic competition among buyers, with *monopsony, duopsony,* or *oligopsony,* according to the number of buyers acting strategically.

The definitions of the particular market structures corresponding to the various entries in the chart are self-evident. The dichotomy introduced between homogeneous and differentiated products is of course more theoretical than real. As we have seen, the extreme case of product homogeneity corresponds to a situation where the smallest price differential drives the entire demand to the cheapest variant. But, apart from this extreme case, infinitesimally small graduations in the degree of differentiation can be introduced, which makes it difficult in practice to identify when homogeneity stops and differentiation starts. Similarly, the distinction between 'few' and 'many' sellers cannot be established in a perfectly dichotomous manner. The essential element here is whether sellers are, or are not, aware of the interactive decision context in which they operate. The oligopolistic structures cover the cases of duopoly, triopoly, etc., according to the number of sellers (two, three, etc.). The case of a single seller (monopoly) has to be distinguished from the others. The reason is that the monopolist has no competitor and is not in an interactive decision context. By contrast, the case of homogeneous monopoly must be distinguished from the case of differentiated monopoly. In the first case, the monopolist sells a single product, while in the second, he sells two or several products which are imperfect substitutes: the monopolist then competes with himself!

The entry in the chart corresponding to the situation of a large number of competitors selling differentiated products (monopolistic competition) calls for special comment. This market structure covers the case where, in spite of the presence of a large number of competitors, each perceives the dependence of his selling price on the quantity he supplies the market. This perception of the relationship between price and quantity supplied follows from the fact that each competitor sells a product which differs from the products sold by the others, even if his own product is a substitute for these others. This market structure postulates however that, due to the large number of competitors, each one is unaware of the strategic context in which he is involved. An example which is often proposed in order to illustrate this situation is the case of retail shopping in a large town. As we shall see (Chapter 3), the two assumptions which characterize this structure (perception by the sellers of the price–quantity relationship and ignorance of the strategic interaction), seem rather incompatible: it seems, indeed, that a seller of a differentiated product should be aware that the quantity demanded for his product depends not only on his own price, but also on prices quoted by some sellers of substitute products.

Among the market structures appearing in the chart above, one may wonder why economists are so very interested in the case of perfect competition. There are several reasons which justify this interest. The first is rather prosaic: the competitive assumptions make it particularly easy to determine the price–quantity market solution. We have illustrated above (see Section 2.1.1) how these assumptions allow an easy identification of the price and the quantity exchanged on a competitive market. The second reason is more subtle and will be evoked several times below. In fact, this structure appears to be the limit case of oligopolistic markets with strategic agents when the number of these agents is increased without bound. Intuitively, their power to influence the market price by their individual action diminishes when this number increases, and tends to disappear completely at the limit. Each seller must then take the price as given, which is precisely the case of perfect competition.

Furthermore, there are political arguments in favour of perfect competition. In particular, the atomistic structure required by the competitive organization of markets guarantees the *decentralization of decision-making* and the *dispersion of power*, two key objectives of the liberal ideology. Finally – and this is the essential reason why economists are interested in perfect competition – it *ensures an efficient allocation of resources in the economy*.

First of all, each firm produces at the competitive solution a quantity of output for which marginal cost is equal to market price. If the price measures the utility obtained by the last consumer who buys the product at that price, then the value of resources used to satisfy the demand of this consumer is exactly equal to the amount of utility created by it. If this had not been the case, for instance if the marginal cost had been strictly smaller than the unit price, it would have been advantageous to increase production by at least one unit: the increase in utility obtained from serving a further consumer would exceed the market value of resources needed for producing this further unit, as measured by its marginal cost. The allocation of resources would then be inefficient. Furthermore, at the long-run competitive equilibrium, average production cost of each firm is equal to market price: the receipts of each firm are just sufficient to cover investment and variable costs allowing production of the selected quantity. Finally, the entry process leads to the elimination of those firms which are less efficient in the production of the good: their production costs exceed those of the firms which are able to survive at equilibrium.

These three properties – equality of price and marginal cost, zero profits and elimination of intramarginal firms – guarantee that resources are efficiently used in the industry. As we shall see later, this is no longer the case under imperfect competition. Strategic interaction between agents introduces distortions in the way resources are allocated in the economy. The study of these distortions, and the political measures needed to circumvent them, is still a widely unexplored domain of research in economic theory.

3

THE NUMBER OF AGENTS: ENTRY, BARRIERS TO ENTRY AND COLLUSION

This chapter examines how the market solution is affected when the first assumption of perfect competition – the large number of agents – is relaxed. After analysing market contexts involving a very small number of (strategic) agents (monopoly, duopoly), we shall consider the consequences of strategic entry of new competitors when entry barriers are absent. In Section 3.2, the problem of strategic entry barriers, organized by incumbent firms with a view to postponing or discouraging entry, will be examined. Finally, in Section 3.3, we study the effects of collusion on the market solution: collusion has the reverse effect of entry on the number of agents since it decreases artificially the number of market decision units. In the same section, we analyse also the inherent unstability of collusive agreements related to the difficulties of coordinating firms' decisions.

3.1 Entry and strategic competition

3.1.1 *A small number of sellers: Monopoly and duopoly*

Before analysing the consequences of entry of new firms on a market with strategic agents, it is interesting to consider the case of homogeneous monopoly and duopoly, in order both to contrast these cases with each other and to introduce the concept of non-cooperative equilibrium in the framework of the classical market model. Consider the following example borrowed from Cournot (1838). The owner of a mineral water source with two branches dies and his two sons inherit the plots of land where these two branches spring out of the ground. Each son receives one branch. The two brothers decide to exploit the source together, exactly as a monopolist would do it. The cost of exploiting each branch is given by

$$C(q) = \frac{1}{3200} + \frac{q^2}{2}, \qquad (3.1)$$

with q denoting the quantity of mineral water bottled at the branch. If they decide to sell a quantity Q the price $p(Q)$ at which this quantity is absorbed by the market is given by the expression

$$p(Q) = 1 - Q. \qquad (3.2)$$

Let us suppose that both brothers know exactly the relationship existing between the market price and the quantity which can be sold at that price. What quantity of mineral water will they decide to sell? If they decide to maximize their joint profit (monopoly profit), they will sell together the quantity of mineral water for which the profit $p(Q) \cdot Q - C(Q)$ is maximal. In our example, the profit is given by the expression :

$$p(Q) \cdot Q - C(Q) = (1 - Q) \cdot Q - \frac{Q^2}{2} - \frac{1}{3200}. \tag{3.3}$$

Differentiating the profit with respect to Q, the optimal value for Q obtains as $Q = Q_M = \frac{1}{3}$. The corresponding profit, obtained by replacing Q_M in the above expression, is equal to $\frac{1}{6} - \frac{1}{3200}$, a strictly positive value covering fixed as well as variable costs. The selling price is equal to $p(Q_M) = p_M = \frac{2}{3}$.

Now suppose that a conflict arises between the two brothers, who decide to cease cooperation and serve the market separately and without coordination. From the viewpoint of market structure, the end of this cooperation means that a non-cooperative duopoly is substituted for the previous monopoly arrangement. Which are the quantities q_1 and q_2 that the two brothers will now decide to produce? To answer this question, let us identify the non-cooperative equilibrium defined above to the particular context of our market game. The set of strategies S of each seller is the unit interval $[0, 1]$: no seller would consider selling more than one, since otherwise the price would be equal to zero. If the first seller chooses the strategy q_1 and the second the strategy q_2, the resulting selling price will be equal to $1 - (q_1 + q_2)$, since $q_1 + q_2$ is now the aggregate supply. Substituting this value for the price in the profit function of each seller, we obtain as payoffs to the pair of strategies (q_1, q_2)

$$\pi_1(q_1, q_2) = (1 - q_1 - q_2) \cdot q_1 - \frac{q_1^2}{2} - \frac{1}{3200} \tag{3.4}$$

for the first and

$$\pi_2(q_1, q_2) = (1 - q_1 - q_2) \cdot q_2 - \frac{q_2^2}{2} - \frac{1}{3200} \tag{3.5}$$

for the second. *We recognize here the interactive decision context* introduced above: the profit of each brother depends of course on his own strategic choice, but also on the strategic choice of his opponent. To determine the non-cooperative equilibrium, it suffices to identify the pair of strategies (q_1^*, q_2^*) such that none of the players has an advantageous deviation from it. Differentiating π_1 with respect to q_1 and π_2 with respect to q_2 and cancelling the derivatives, we obtain the linear system:

$$q_1 = \frac{1 - q_2}{3} \tag{3.6}$$

$$q_2 = \frac{1 - q_1}{3}, \tag{3.7}$$

the solution of which is given by $q_1^* = q_2^* = \frac{1}{4}$; the pair of strategies $(\frac{1}{4}, \frac{1}{4})$ is the non-cooperative equilibrium of this duopoly market. As for the price $p(q_1^*, q_2^*)$, it is now equal to $\frac{1}{2}$: the market price has decreased from $\frac{2}{3}$ to $\frac{1}{2}$ due to the absence of cooperation between the brothers!

When comparing monopoly with duopoly, we identify three major differences between the market solutions corresponding to each of these market structures. First of all, and we have already stressed this point above, monopoly does not correspond to a context of interactive decision-making: the monopolist does not compete with anybody! By contrast, the decisions of the duopolists are interdependent: each duopolist is conscious that his profit depends not only on his own strategy, but also on the strategy of his opponent. It is in fact the above difference which induces the two others: in duopoly the price is lower and the quantity larger than in monopoly. These two properties are akin to those observed under entry when firms behave competitively. Remember that entry of a new firm in a competitive market decreases the market price and increases the quantity exchanged (see Section 2.1). But there is an important difference between the two phenomena even if their effects are the same. In pure competition the new entrant, like the incumbent firms, will behave as a price-taker, while in duopoly both agents take into account their strategic interaction and its consequences on price formation when deciding about their individual supply.

Another important point must be stressed concerning the non-cooperative theory of duopoly. In the above analysis we have assumed that in their rivalry, duopolists use *quantities* as strategies in order to influence the market outcome. But we could just as well have assumed that duopolists enter into *price* competition, each serving all customers desiring to buy from him at the announced price. Under this alternative assumption, strategies are prices, and one may wonder whether the non-cooperative equilibrium obtained with the use of price strategies coincides with that resulting from using quantities as strategies. This question was raised by Bertrand (1883) after reading the book by Cournot.

Simple reasoning, already sketched above, shows that the conclusion to the above conjecture is negative. If all potential buyers share full information about prices selected by the duopolists, they will want to buy from the seller quoting the lowest price. Accordingly, the duopolist with the higher price has zero demand and is obliged to lower his price below that announced by his competitor in order to win back customers. This process will continue as long as this price war does not cancel out the profits of both sellers: the non-cooperative equilibrium with price strategies corresponds to the pair of prices at which each duopolist makes zero profit! *Strategic price competition, even with a small number of sellers, leads spontaneously to the competitive solution!* This conclusion is often corroborated by facts since price wars are often observed when the sellers of a homogeneous good cannot organize collusive agreements among them.

Who is right in the debate between Bertrand and Cournot? Do firms use quantity or price strategies in order to influence the market outcome? One way to reconcile the two viewpoints consists of assuming that firms use both strategies, but in a sequential way. This is the approach suggested by Kreps and Scheinkman (1983). The choice of quantity is perceived as a choice of productive capacity;

then quantity is chosen before price, since the latter can be adjusted more easily than the former. Firms determine non-cooperatively their capacity in a first stage, taking into account the consequence of this choice on the ensuing price competition. Then, given their capacities, they select, also non-cooperatively, their price. Kreps and Scheinkman show that the non-cooperative equilibrium of this sequential game has the Cournot outcome as capacity choice for each firm.

3.1.2 *Strategic entry*

The analysis proposed by Cournot provides a market solution when sellers are few and act non-cooperatively. Now we must extend this analysis to the case of an arbitrary number of agents adopting a similar non-cooperative behaviour. This extension will allow us, on the one hand, to examine the effects of strategic entry and, on the other, to compare these effects with those which would follow from 'competitive entry', with price-taking entrants. To proceed in that direction, let us consider first an increase in the number of sellers in the Cournot example of the mineral water market studied above. In a more abstract way, let us now suppose that the industry includes a number n of sellers, each of whom has the same cost structure as either of our two duopolists. We start with the analysis of *competitive entry*, in which each seller takes the market price as given. Thus each seller maximizes the expression

$$\pi(q) = pq - \frac{q^2}{2} - \frac{1}{3200},$$

which generates an individual supply function $s(p) = p$, with an aggregate supply equal to $S(p) = np$. The equality of supply $S(p)$ and demand $D(p) = 1-p$ implies that $1 - p = np$, so that the equilibrium price is equal to $\frac{1}{n+1}$. At that price each individual firm supplies $\frac{1}{n+1}$ and realizes a profit equal to $\frac{1}{2(n+1)^2} - \frac{1}{3200}$. It is easily checked that this profit is positive if and only if the number of firms is less than 39. It is equal to 0 when $n = 39$, which is the highest number of firms which can coexist on this competitive market. When there are exactly 39 firms, each produces a quantity at which average cost is minimal, and each makes zero profit.

The theory just proposed rests on the assumption that sellers take the market price as given, whatever the number n of competitors operating in the market-place. But what are the consequences of entry when sellers explicitly take into account their strategic interaction? When n is equal to 2, we already know the answer: we observe a duopoly, as described in the preceding section. When n is greater than 2, it is not difficult to extend the above duopoly approach to the corresponding case. Let n be any integer representing the number of sellers operating in the market, and q_i the quantity supplied strategically by seller i, $i = 1, \ldots, n$. A *non-cooperative equilibrium* with n sellers is defined as a n-tuple of quantities q_i^*, one for each seller i, such that, considering the strategies q_j, $j = 1, \ldots, n$, $j \neq i$, as fixed, no seller i can unilaterally increase his profit by deviating from q_i^*, the quantity chosen at equilibrium. Now the firms do not take the market price as given, since each one of them knows that this price explicitly depends on his own strategic supply q_i, and on the aggregate supply $\sum_{\substack{j=1 \\ j \neq i}}^{n} q_j$ of the other sellers. The profit of firm i is then given by

$$\pi_i \left(q_i, \sum_{j \neq i} q_j \right) = \left(1 - \sum_{j \neq i} q_j - q_i \right) q_i - \frac{q_i^2}{2} - \frac{1}{3200}. \tag{3.8}$$

Each oligopolist maximizes his profit with respect to q_i, the q_js being considered as given. Differentiating the profit of firm i with respect to q_i and cancelling the derivative, we obtain the linear system:

$$q_i = \frac{1 - \sum_{j \neq i} q_j}{3}; i = 1, \ldots, n. \tag{3.9}$$

Since all firms face the same problem, the simultaneous solution of system (3.9) implies that $q_i = q_j$ for all i and j, that is, all firms supply an identical quantity at equilibrium, say q^*. It is easy to find the explicit value of q^* by solving the system (3.9) with $q_i = q_j$ for all i and j, that is

$$q^* = \frac{1}{n+2};$$

we see immediately that this 'general' solution coincides with the solution we found for the particular case $n = 2$, namely, $q^* = \frac{1}{4}$.

It follows from the above that at equilibrium with n strategic firms, each produces a quantity which is smaller than the quantity this firm would supply in a competitive market (remember that, in the same example with n competitive firms, each supplies a quantity $s(p)$ equal to $\frac{1}{n+1}$), and sells this quantity at a price $p_D = \frac{2}{n+2}$, which exceeds the competitive price $\frac{1}{n+1}$. Nevertheless, *when the number of entrants increases, the profits of incumbent firms are also eroded, as under perfect competition*. However, the profit of each firm becomes negative for a number of firms which exceeds the number of firms at which competitive firms have zero profits: in our example, it can be verified that this number is equal to 67. This compares with 40 firms under competitive entry. This conclusion is not surprising since the quantity sold by each firm for $n = 67$ ($\frac{1}{69}$) is smaller than the quantity for which average cost is minimal ($\frac{1}{40}$). It can be shown that the properties of profit erosion and overcapacity with strategic entry are very generally satisfied at a quantity oligopoly equilibrium (for more details, see Friedman 1983: Chapter 2).

Before looking at the methods which can be used by firms to mitigate profit erosion due to entry, it is useful to examine the consequences, on resource allocation, of competition 'among the few'. In the case of monopoly, we have deduced that the price is equal to $\frac{2}{3}$ (see Section 3.1.1, p. 31). Substituting the corresponding quantity $Q_M = \frac{1}{3}$ into the marginal cost function $\frac{dC}{dQ} = Q$ of the monopolist, we see that the monopoly price exceeds the marginal cost of Q_M. Consequently, the *optimality condition for allocative efficiency, which requires the equality of marginal cost and price, is not satisfied at the monopoly solution*: the cost of increasing production by one unit is smaller than the utility derived by the consumer who would buy that unit at price p_M.

In the case of duopoly, the price p_D is equal to $\frac{1}{2}$ and the marginal cost of the quantity $q_1^* = q_2^* = \frac{1}{4}$ produced by each duopolist is also equal to $\frac{1}{4}$. In this case also there exists a discrepancy between price and marginal cost so that the optimality condition is again violated. Nonetheless, this discrepancy is weaker under duopoly than under monopoly: even if entry has not realized the optimality condition, it has reduced the distorsion resulting from the existence of a single seller in monopoly.

One can easily check that the discrepancy between marginal cost and price decreases in proportion as the number of firms entering the market increases. However, for the number of firms at which none makes a profit in the case of *strategic entry* (67), marginal cost of production ($\frac{1}{69}$) is still strictly smaller than price ($\frac{2}{69}$): again, this is not surprising since the quantity sold by each firm is smaller than the quantity corresponding to minimum average cost. By contrast, under *competitive entry*, each firm produces at the long-run equilibrium the quantity corresponding to minimum average cost ($\frac{1}{40}$). In conclusion, even assuming free entry of firms in the industry, strategic behaviour leads to significant distortions in resource allocation. But these distortions can even be amplified when incumbent firms select specific strategies in order to avoid the negative prospects of existing, or potential, competition.

3.2 Barriers to entry and competition

3.2.1 *The theory of limit pricing*

The theory of strategic entry which we have just examined assumes that incumbent firms select their strategies without anticipating that later entry will occur. However, excepting the case of pure monopoly or natural monopoly, there is room for entry as long as the profit of incumbent firms has not been completely eroded. It must be expected however that firms which occupied the market at the very beginning of the entry process will practise policies in order to discourage entry: this may prevent profit erosion by potential candidates to entry. In other words, incumbents tend to erect *strategic barriers*. To simplify the analysis, consider again a monopoly supplying the quantity at which its profit is maximal. In Fig. 3.1(a), the curve $LRAC$ represents the long-run average cost curve while the curve mC represents the marginal cost as a function of the quantity Q. The line DD' is the demand function expressing, for each level of Q, the price $p(Q)$ at which the quantity Q is absorbed by the market. The line mR is the marginal receipt. At the profit-maximizing level of output, Q_M, marginal receipts equal marginal cost; the selling price is p_M. Now consider a potential competitor with the same technology as the incumbent monopolist, and accordingly facing the same production costs. If this firm enters the market, there is no reason why

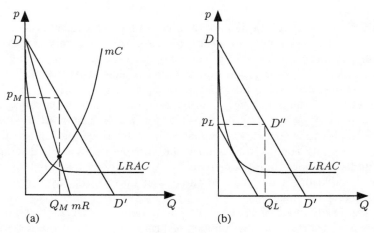

FIG. 3.1.

it cannot obtain positive profits if it supplies a quantity q whose average cost remains smaller than $p(Q_M + q)$. Accordingly, without any self-protecting ma-noeuvre by the monopolist, he will now be exposed to the competitive threat of the entrant. A more sophisticated behaviour could be the following. *If the entrant is convinced that the incumbent will not change his output level after entry,* it is sufficient for the latter to select a quantity Q_L for which, at the resulting price $p_L = p(Q_L)$, the entrant cannot make a positive profit, whatever the quantity he is considering supplying. Then entry is barred because it is no longer attractive to the entrant firm. To select the quantity Q_L, the monopolist must proceed in such a way that for any quantity q of the entrant, the long-run average cost of q, $LRAC(q)$, exceeds the price $p(Q_L + q)$. To identify the values Q_L and $p(Q_L)$, it is useful to refer to Fig. 3.1(b). If the monopolist elects to sell Q_L at price p_L, the 'residual' demand still available for the candidate to entry is given by the segment $D''D'$. Since we have assumed that the latter has the same technology as the incumbent, he is also facing the same $LRAC(q)$, and we notice that, for any quantity q the entrant sold, the resulting price $p(Q_L + q)$ cannot cover the long-run average cost $LRAC(q)$. Consequently, Q_L and p_L succeed in barring entry. The price p_L is called the *limit price*: it is the highest price that the mo-nopolist can quote while guaranteeing that the entrant cannot make any positive profit. The assumption according to which the entrant is convinced before entry that the incumbent firm will not change its output level, is known as the *Sylos Labini postulate* (see Sylos Labini 1957). The limit pricing theory rests on a very simple idea. If the entrant anticipates an output inertia from the incumbent after entry, the latter can always prevent entry by increasing ex-ante output so that the price decreases below average cost, should entry occur.

3.2.2   *The role of investment as a barrier to entry*

The main criticism of the theory of limit pricing is related to the Sylos Labini postulate: why should the potential entrants have precisely the conjectures postulated by this theory? And why should the monopolist lend these conjectures to the potential entrants? A more plausible assumption is that they would anticipate a non-cooperative competition with the incumbent firm, should they decide to enter. In this case, the anticipations of the entrant about the output reaction of the incumbent *after* entry are no longer necessarily fixed, as postulated by Sylos Labini, but may depend on the output choice of the incumbent firm *before* entry.

Consider for instance a market in which firm 1 decides to enter, but anticipates that, in the next period, another firm – say, firm 2 – will contemplate the possibility of entry. Since firm 1 enters before firm 2, it can signal to the latter the quantity of the product it intends to produce, should firm 2 decide to enter. In particular, the choice of a productive *capacity* can serve as a signal indicating to the potential entrant the output that the incumbent firm intends to produce at the non-cooperative equilibrium which will arise after entry. If, indeed, a non-cooperative equilibrium is reached after entry, and if this non-cooperative equilibrium depends on the capacity decision of firm 1, it can possibly adapt this capacity so as to discourage, *ex ante*, the potential entrant: the initial investment can be so important that the profits expected from entry by firm 2 at the resulting non-cooperative equilibrium, no longer justify entry.

Dixit (1980) has proposed an analysis which formalizes the above mechanism relating investment to entry barriers. He considers two firms, firm 1 being the incumbent and firm 2 the potential entrant. Their cost structures are identical and given by $C(x,k) = f + wx + rk$, where f is a set-up cost independent of the level of output, r the average cost of capacity k and w the unit cost of production x. The rules of the game are as follows. Firm 1 chooses a capacity level k_1 before the entry of firm 2; this level can be later increased, but not decreased. If firm 2 decides to enter, both firms choose their production levels x_1 and x_2 at the corresponding non-cooperative equilibrium. If there is no entry, firm 1 remains monopolist. First notice that the choice of capacity k_1 determines the marginal cost function of firm 1. When $x_1 < k_1$, the marginal cost of x_1 is equal to w; but when the selected output level x_1 exceeds capacity k_1, the latter must be simultaneously increased so that the marginal cost now becomes equal to $w + r$ (see Fig. 3.2). It follows that the output choice of firm 1 facing a supply x_2 from the entrant also depends on the selected capacity k_1. Indeed, this choice must maximize with respect to x_1 the profit $\pi(x_1 + x_2) \cdot x_1 - C(x_1, k_1)$, with $\pi(x_1 + x_2)$ denoting the price at which the quantity $(x_1 + x_2)$ can be sold: clearly this maximization implies the equality of marginal receipt and marginal cost. As a function of the output level x_2, this equality can obtain at an output level x_1 which is either smaller than capacity k_1, or which exceeds this capacity. In the first case the marginal cost is equal to w, while in the second it is equal to $w + r$. In Fig. 3.2 the graph of the marginal cost function is superimposed upon

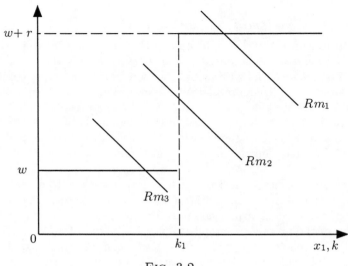

FIG. 3.2.

the marginal receipt functions Rm_1, Rm_2, and Rm_3 of firm 1 corresponding to three different levels of production of firm 2: the lower x_2 is, the more to the north-east the marginal receipt function of firm 1 will be, since the residual demand to firm 1 increases when x_2 decreases. When firm 2 selects a level of output generating a marginal receipt function like Rm_1 or Rm_2, the marginal cost is then equal to w at the optimal output for firm 1 at which marginal cost is equal to marginal receipt; when the production level of firm 2 generates a marginal receipt like Rm_1, the marginal cost is then equal to $w+r$ at the optimal output level of firm 1. Accordingly, this optimal output of the incumbent firm against the level of production selected by the entrant depends on the capacity k_1 selected by the incumbent in period 1. In particular, since the equilibrium output x_1^* corresponding to the non-cooperative equilibrium (x_1^*, x_2^*) obtains as the profit-maximizing output against x_2^*, the non-cooperative equilibrium of the game after entry depends itself on the choice of capacity decided by firm 1 before entry occurs. *As a consequence, firm 1 can manipulate, via its choice of capacity, the non-cooperative equilibrium which would be realized, should firm 2 decide to enter; and, accordingly, the profits realized by firm 2 at this equilibrium.*

Nevertheless, this strategic use of capacity is costly for firm 1, which has to make a tradeoff between the advantage of maintaining a monopolistic position by preventing the entry of firm 2, and the additional cost generated by the excess capacity required to prevent this entry. Dixit shows that, according to the size of the market and the importance of fixed costs, sometimes it is profitable for firm 1 to select a level of capacity preventing the entry of firm 2, and sometimes profitable to accommodate entry by choosing a smaller level of capacity.

3.2.3 *Dynamic limit pricing*

In the above formulation of the limit pricing theory, entry is presented as if the incumbent is facing the only alternative of barring entry or accommodating it. At a price lower than or equal to the limit price, the threat of entry is eliminated; at a higher price, entry takes place immediately. This approach can be criticized on the basis that entry of new firms in an industry can also be viewed as a dynamic process in which the rate of entry increases with the price used by the incumbent. If this price is high, the potential entrants expect to obtain significant profits if they decide to enter, so that a significant number of them will be attracted. In proportion as this price is progressively lowered, expected profits decrease and a smaller and smaller number of firms will remain interested in invading the market: the rate of entry decreases.

Anticipating the entry process, the incumbent firm can manipulate the rate of entry. Immediate profitability calls for a high price, but in practice may decrease future profitability since a high price today increases the rate at which the industry attracts new competitors. The incumbent firm must accordingly select the price trajectory which maximizes the discounted sum of all future profits. There is no reason why the corresponding optimal trajectory leads the firm to apply the limit price policy today. It may prefer to start with the monopoly price, and accept that monopoly profits are progressively eroded as a consequence of a high entry rate: this strategy can be particularly advantageous when the discount rate is high, or when uncertainty concerning future demand is important. Furthermore, between the two extreme policies consisting of either barring immediate entry by using the limit price, or setting the monopoly price and accepting entry, all intermediate policies have to be taken into account. These consist of modulating the rate of entry according to the price $p(t)$ selected at each time t on the trajectory. When $p(t)$ increases, the entry rate increases, and vice versa.

Gaskins (1971) has proposed a dynamic model allowing the analysis of the optimal price trajectory. He considers a market occupied by an incumbent firm, facing a fringe of potential competitors who would be willing to invade the market if profits were sufficiently attractive. He assumes that these competitors adjust optimally their production at time t, taking as given the price $p(t)$ decided by the incumbent. It follows that the total amount $X(t)$ sold by this competitive fringe increases (decreases) as $p(t)$ increases (decreases). Gaskins assumes that the variation of $X(t)$ is proportional to the discrepancy between the price $p(t)$ and the price p_0 equal to the minimum average cost of the entrants, that is

$$\frac{dX}{dt} = k(p(t) - p_0), \tag{3.10}$$

where k denotes the coefficient of proportionality. The incumbent firm has the possibility of modifying the rate of entry $\frac{dX}{dt}$ by adapting the trajectory $p(t)$ as time evolves; $p(t)$ is the *control variable* and $X(t)$ the *state variable*. The objective function of the firm is to maximize the discounted sum of future profits by selecting the optimal price trajectory $p(t)$.

Gaskins proves that there exists a solution to the above optimal control problem, and analyses how this solution depends on the main parameters: demand, the incumbent average cost and the price p_0. In some cases, the optimal trajectory leads the incumbent to delay entry: the firm accepts its market share to be progressively eroded by the competitive fringe. Then the market price $p(t)$ tends, with t, to the competitive price. In other cases, it is optimal for the incumbent to opt, from the very beginning, for a pricing strategy excluding the possibility of entry for the candidates: then $p(t)$ is immediately set below the minimum average cost p_0 of potential rivals. This is, in particular, the case when the incumbent benefits from an absolute cost advantage over them.

Gaskins's analysis is not without its faults. First, it is unclear about the reasons which motivate the entry decision of the firms in the fringe: no formal analysis is provided which could explane this decision since the entry equation (3.10) is given exogenously. Furthermore, even if the incumbent behaves rationally when faced with this entry process, it is also unclear why the incumbent keeps the power of setting the market price after entry of the competitors. Most probably one should expect them to be willing to participate in the price formation process. On the other hand, the entry rate at time t, as specified by equation (3.10), only depends on the current price $p(t)$. Most probably, however, candidates to entry base their entry decision not on the current price, but on the price they expect to prevail after entry. This assumption of myopia seems difficult to swallow.

We have examined in this section how incumbent firms can take advantage of being the first to operate in the industry, either by barring entry to potential entrants, or by controling profit erosion resulting from strategic entry. These policies aim at wiping out the negative effects of potential competition. But, even assuming that, in spite of their efforts, entry has taken place, still the possibility remains of neutralizing, or at least attenuating these effects, by 'combining' among them. We refer now to collusive agreements through which firms coordinate their price or output policies.

3.3   Collusion and competition

3.3.1   *The difficulties of coordination*

The example provided in Chapter 2 (Section 2.1.3) clearly identifies the advantages firms can obtain from price or output coordination: by imposing adequately chosen production quotas on its members, the cooperative of corn producers succeeds in raising the selling price above the level resulting from free competition. Whenever the sellers recognize their mutual interaction, there is room for beneficial cooperation. Indeed joint profits always exceed the sum of profits that they can realize by acting individually: the non-cooperative solution can always be reached by mutual agreement! Consider for instance a quantity duopoly game, with q_1 denoting the quantity sold by the first duopolist, q_2 the quantity sold by the second, $C(q)$ the total cost function of each of them and $p(q_1 + q_2)$ the market demand function for the product. The profit of seller 1, π_1, is given by

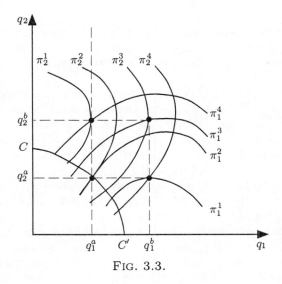

$$\text{FIG. 3.3.}$$

$$\pi_1(q_1, q_2) = p(q_1 + q_2) \cdot q_1 - C(q_1)$$

and that of seller 2 by

$$\pi_2(q_1, q_2) = p(q_1 + q_2) \cdot q_2 - C(q_2).$$

Figure 3.3 shows the isoprofit curves of the two sellers in the plane. For instance, the curve π_1^1 identifies the (q_1, q_2) pairs corresponding to the same level of profit, π_1^1, for firm 1. This locus changes for different levels of profits. For instance, the curve π_1^2 corresponds to pairs (q_1, q_2) giving lower profits to firm 1 than those lying on the curve π_1^1: for each level q_1 on the latter, firm 2 sells more output than on the former, and the residual demand to be served by firm 1 is smaller and leads accordingly to a smaller profit. Similarly, the isoprofit curves of firm 2 correspond to smaller and smaller levels of profit in proportion as they move to the east in Fig. 3.3. The points at which two isoprofit curves are tangential, like the point (q_1^a, q_2^a) in Fig. 3.3, enjoy a remarkable property: starting from such a point, it is impossible to find another pair of outputs at which the profit of both firms is simultaneously increased. Here we recognize the idea of a cooperative equilibrium which we introduced in Section 2.4. Consequently, the locus of these points (the curve CC') corresponds to the set of cooperative equilibria of the duopoly game: this locus is called the *contract curve*.

When firms succeed in coordinating their output decisions, they will certainly select a point on the contract curve, but which one? If the two firms are identical, one should expect each one to select half the quantity which would have been chosen by a monopolist operating on the same market, namely, the point (q_1^a, q_2^a) in Fig. 3.3. It seems a priori that there should be no difficulty in agreeing on a collusive agreement. There exists a clear motivation, since cooperation entails higher profits for both firms than at the non-cooperative equilibrium. Further-more, sharing equally the monopoly profit provides a simple rule to select a particular cooperative equilibrium on the contract curve when both firms are identical.

Nevertheless, there are several reasons why coordination among sellers, which is necessary to fix a collusive agreement and maintain it through time, does not obtain so easily. First, the collusive agreement is essentially fragile: the parties do not ignore the possibility that, once the agreement is signed, all of them could take advantage from secretly breaking its rules. We have already evoked this difficulty in Chapter 2 and we shall come back to it in Section 3.3.2, which is devoted to the problem of stability of collusive agreements. As for the other reasons, they are mainly concerned with the difficulties of reaching an agreement, when the assumption of identical firms is dropped.

To start with, consider the difficulty caused by the asymmetry, among firms, of their cost conditions. When production costs differ, it is far more difficult to obtain an agreement on the division of joint profits. Joint profit maximization then requires that firms produce different levels of output and realize accordingly different levels of individual profits. Perhaps it could even be required that a firm taking part in the agreement closes its doors! When side payments are forbidden by law, it is easy to see that the difficulty of reaching an agreement on the divi-sion of profits can compromise the whole issue of collusion. Furthermore, when firms do not sell a perfectly homogeneous product, it reinforces the difficulty of reaching an agreement about prices or quotas of production. Other asymmetries among firms can also exist. For instance, when incumbent firms collude with a view to preventing entry, they can perceive differently the manner of discount-ing the future, some of them preferring high profits immediately, while others prefer to attach greater weight to long-run benefits. The former would favour a price policy with a high price in the beginning, even if it induces a high rate of entry in the present, while the latter would prefer a limit price policy in order to restrain entry in the short run. Another asymmetry can arise from the fact that firms have different perceptions about the level of future demand. To reach an agreement, firms must also compare their likelihood judgements about events which can influence the level of their future profits, such as technological change, entry of substitute products or other market contingencies. These comparisons can generate conflict among firms trying to accomplish a collusive agreement.

Finally, antitrust rules constitute a major impediment to the willingness of firms to enter into collusion. Then they must get round the law, which can be accepted by some firms but rejected by others. All the above reasons can explain the difficulties encountered by firms when they try to pass a collusive agreement. But this is nothing compared with the difficulties met in maintaining the agreement once it is signed!

3.3.2 *The stability of collusive agreements*

Let us come back for a moment to Fig. 3.3, and suppose that the two firms have agreed to limit their respective production levels to the quotas q_1^a and q_2^a, and to share the resulting monopoly profit. The corresponding profit levels are π_1^2 for firm 1 and π_2^2 for firm 2, respectively. Now suppose that firm 1, speculating on the fact that firm 2 will maintain the quota, decides to increase its production to q_1^b: producing the quantity q_1^b provides a profit π_1^1 to firm 1, the highest attainable profit for this firm, given that firm 2 sticks to its quota. It is clear that $\pi_1^1 > \pi_1^2$, so that there exists a clear incentive for firm 1 to 'cheat' when firm 2 sticks to its quota. Similar reasoning applies to firm 2 under the assumption that firm 1 keeps its production at the level decided in the agreement: supplying q_2^b provides a profit π_1^2, $\pi_1^2 > \pi_2^2$, to firm 2. But Fig. 3.3 also reveals that, when a firm anticipates that its rival will cheat, it is also to its advantage to cheat! For instance, assuming that firm 2 cheats and supplies q_2^b, it is better for firm 1 to cheat and produce q_1^b than to maintain the quota q_1^a, since the profit realized in the first alternative is equal to π_1^3 and exceeds the profit π_1^4 obtained in the second. It follows that, in all circumstances – whether the opponent cheats or maintains the quota – each firm is always better off when cheating! The situation analysed here is completely analogous to the 'box game' examined in Section 2.3.2, in which each player prefers to put nothing in the box, because whatever the strategy selected by the opponent, the highest payoff obtains when nothing is put in the box.

The alternatives offered to the firms in the 'cartel game' can also be represented by a payoff matrix, with two strategies for each firm: 'maintain the quota' and 'cheat', and entries corresponding to the pair of profits obtained by the firms when using these strategies (for instance the entry (4,4) corresponds to the level of profit of the firms obtained at the cooperative equilibrium (q_1^a, q_2^a) and the entry (1,5) to the profits when firm 1 sticks to the quota q_1^a and firm 2 elects to cheat by selling q_2^b. It is easy to check that each firm's optimal strategy is to

Firm 1 \ Firm 2	Maintain the quota	Cheat
Maintain the quota	(4,4)	(1,5)
Cheat	(5,1)	(3,3)

'cheat', whatever the strategy selected by its rival. Consequently, we must conclude that, once it is signed, the cartel agreement is immediately threatened by destabilizing forces, as described above. Without an enforceable contract, there is little chance that it could be maintained. But such contracts are generally illegal, due to antitrust policies preventing collusion of firms operating in the same industrial sector.

Then one may wonder why such agreements are *de facto* observed, even if their existence is not explicitly recognized. This is because collusion can be tacit and follows, paradoxical as it may appear at first sight, from a non-cooperative behaviour. The intuition of this result is due to Chamberlin 1933: 48

> If each seller seeks his maximum profit rationally and intelligently, he will realize that when there are only two or a few sellers, his own move has a considerable effect upon his competitors, and that it makes it idle to suppose that they will accept without retaliation the losses he forces upon them. Since the result of a cut by any one is inevitably to decrease his own profits, no one will cut, and although the sellers are entirely independent, the equilibrium result is the same as though there were a monopolistic agreement between them.

It is not difficult to provide a rigorous explanation of Chamberlin's intuition using the conceptual framework of game theory. Suppose, indeed, that the cartel game defined above is played repeatedly *ad infinitum*: at each period of time, the two firms select separately one of the two strategies 'maintain the quota' or 'cheat'. In the infinitely repeated game a strategy is then defined as an infinite sequence of such moves, and its payoff as the (discounted) sum of payoffs of the one-shot games played at each period. Suppose that each firm decides unilaterally to stick at any period to the strategy 'maintain the quota', which is equivalent to playing cooperatively at each stage of the infinitely repeated game. Let us show that this pair of strategies constitutes a *non-cooperative* equilibrium of the infinitely repeated game.

If one of the firms decides to deviate at some period from this strategy by electing instead to 'cheat', its rival can punish the deviant by selecting in turn the same strategy for all future periods. It is evident that the transitory increase in payoffs resulting from the deviation cannot compensate for the losses resulting from the eternal punishment imposed by the rival. Accordingly, the deviation cannot generate a higher flow of discounted future profits, and infinitely repeated cooperation appears as a non-cooperative equilibrium of the repeated game! The repetition of the strategic context in which firms operate creates the possibility of retorting practices which could be exercised if one of them deviated from cooperative participation. This threat then constrains each firm to stick to cooperative moves, even if each of them would benefit instantaneously by deviating from the collusive agreement.

This 'constrained cooperation' much resembles behaviour observed during the cold war. Both the Soviet Union and the United States had a short-run advantage in employing the nuclear bomb. But the threat of retortion was sufficient to prevent each of the parties from using it effectively. Thus the potential long-term consequences of a transitory failure of cooperation stabilize a long-term cooperative arrangement, even if the latter is made fragile by the permanent temptation for each party to deviate from it in order to benefit from the short-term advantage of cheating. In reality, some intermediate situations are probably observed. Most certainly firms are aware of the interest they have in cooperating with each other. The threat of retortion prevents them from deviating from cooperation as long as new circumstances, such as a change in the level of demand or the entry of new competitors, do not make deviation more attractive. During the ensuing transitory period, a price war is observed, entailing considerable losses to firms. This induces them to come back to a wiser attitude in which they benefit again from the fruits of cooperation.

We have examined in this chapter how firms can escape the pressure of competition, whether this pressure comes from potential entry or from mutual rivalry. Strategic entry barriers erected by existing firms allow them to fight against potential competition, while price coordination shelters them, at least for some time, from the prejudices of their mutual rivalry. But these are not the only weapons which can be used by firms to prevent profit erosion resulting from competition. They also enjoy the possibility of differentiating their products, thereby making a price war less attractive since they then benefit from 'local' monopoly power. The next chapter is devoted to the study of this possibility.

4

PRODUCT DIFFERENTIATION

In this chapter we abandon the assumption of a homogeneous product to tackle the problem of competition among firms selling *differentiated* products. In Section 4.1 we study the role of product differentiation in the case of monopoly. We consider successively a monopolist selecting a ladder of substitute products, or selecting the quality of a particular good. We come back to strategic competition in Section 4.2 when analysing duopoly under the assumption that the rivals select not only the price of their product, but also the product itself. The two cases of horizontal and vertical differentiation are considered: horizontal differentiation corresponds to the case of spatial competition, while vertical differentiation deals with quality competition. Section 4.3 is devoted to the problem of *entry* in a differentiated market; entry is also distinguished according to whether it takes place on a horizontally or vertically differentiated market.

4.1 Monopoly and product differentiation

4.1.1 *Selecting the product line*

Among the various market structures presented in the matrix of Section 2.4.2, one of the entries corresponds to *differentiated monopoly*. This market structure represents a situation in which a single seller presents for sale several variants of the same product. This raises the question of identifying the optimal number of variants and the price constellation at which these variants should be sold. As an illustration, consider a firm which is a monopoly for the production of cars in some mythical country. It can produce and sell blue and red cars at a unit production cost c assumed to be equal to £50, which is independent of the particular colour of the car. The population of customers falls into two categories. The first includes 200 persons who prefer red cars to blue cars and would be willing to pay £150 for a red car, but only £100 for a blue one. Conversely, the second category includes only customers who prefer the blue car to the red one; it consists of 100 persons who would be willing to pay £60 for a blue car and £50 for a red one. Taking into account this structure of tastes, what is the optimal strategy for the monopolist? To sell red cars to the first category and blue ones to the second, or rather to select one of the two colours, and sell it to the whole population or to a subset of it only?

If the monopolist chooses the first alternative, he quotes a price of £60 for a blue car, which is the reservation price[1] of the second category of consumers, those who are willing to buy a blue car at that price. But notice that the first category of consumers is also willing to buy a blue car at that price, and they will effectively do it as long as the price of a red car exceeds £110 (for instance if the price of a red car were £120, they would obtain a surplus equal to $150-120 = £30$ if they bought a red car and a surplus of $100-60 = £40$ if they bought a blue one, so that all would buy the latter). Thus, given that the price of a blue car is equal to £60, the highest price that the first category of consumers would be willing to pay for a red car is £110. The profit realized when choosing the first option is thus equal to $(200 \times 110) + (100 \times 60) - 300c = £28\,000 - £15\,000 = £13\,000$. Now assume that the monopolist selects the second possibility and decides to sell only red cars to the first category of consumers. Then he can sell them at a unit price of £150, since he does not compete now with the blue cars which have been withdrawn from the market. Then his profit is equal to $(150 \times 200) - 200c = £30\,000 - £10\,000 = £20\,000$, which substantially exceeds the profit realized under the first alternative. The optimal solution for the monopolist is thus to sell only red cars, and only to those consumers who prefer red cars to blue ones.

In the case of a homogeneous product, we have already drawn the attention of the reader to the distortion generated by monopoly: the discrepancy between the marginal cost of production and price reveals a misallocation of resources resulting from market power. We have just exhibited another type of distortion which can be observed under monopoly: *nothing guarantees that the monopolist will select the variants of the product which would be optimal from the viewpoint of the consumers.* In the particular case we have just analysed, consumers would have been better off if the monopolist had sold red cars to those who prefer red cars, and blue cars to those who prefer blue ones; furthermore, total costs would have been the same, since the unit cost of a car has been assumed to be independent of its colour. It is clear that a competitive market would have realized this scheme: all cars would have been sold at marginal cost c and at that price consumers would have elected to buy their preferred colour. As for the monopolist, not only does he choose a price which exceeds by far the marginal cost of production, but he excludes from consumption a group of consumers without any justification founded on cost reduction.

The above example is one among many possible illustrations of inadequacies which can be observed when product selection is operated by monopoly. In this example, too little variety is offered; but it can also be the case that the monopolist selects a variety of products which is too diversified, compared to the diversity required by welfare maximization (on this point, see Tirole 1988).

4.1.2 *Quality selection*

A similar problem arises when the monopolist selects the level of quality of the product he decides to sell: does he spontaneously select a quality which would

---

[1]The term 'reservation price' is a technical term meaning 'the highest price a consumer would be willing to pay for an object'.

be optimal from the viewpoint of the consumers? It is not difficult to build an example showing that the monopolist is led to choose a quality level which is not optimal from their viewpoint. To this end, consider that he can select one of two variants of a given product. The first variant has a unit production cost c_1 equal to 1, the second a cost c_2 equal to 3. The second variant is assumed to be of a higher quality: all consumers prefer variant 2 to variant 1. Suppose that the population of consumers is composed of two individuals; $\pi_1 = 10$ and $\pi_2 = 11$ are the reservation prices of the first consumer for one unit of variant 1 and 2, respectively. Similarly, $\pi'_1 = 1$ and $\pi'_2 = 5$ are the reservation prices of the second consumer for the two variants. Since $\pi_1 < \pi_2$ and $\pi'_1 < \pi'_2$, the second variant is preferred to the first one. Furthermore, even taking into account the production costs differential, it is still better from the viewpoint of consumers that variant 2 be selected by the monopolist. We observe, indeed, that if this variant is sold at unit cost, total consumer surplus is equal to $\pi_2 + \pi'_2 - 2c_2 = 10$, while if variant 1 is sold in the same conditions, total surplus is only equal to $\pi_1 + \pi_2 - 2c_1 = 9$.

It is easy to show, however, that, when guided by profit maximization, the monopolist sells the low-quality variant 1, and does it to a single consumer only. The available alternatives are either to sell the high-quality variant to both consumers, or to sell it to consumer 2 only, or to sell the low-quality one to both consumers, or to consumer 1 only. In the first alternative, he must set the price of variant 2 equal to 5 for, otherwise, consumer 2 would not be willing to buy it; then he realizes a profit equal to $10 - 6 = 4$. In the second alternative, he may sell it at a price equal to 11, from which the cost must be deducted, leading to a profit equal to 8. When he sells variant 1 to both consumers, he cannot quote a price for variant 1 which would exceed 1 for, otherwise, consumer 2 would not be willing to buy it: this cannot be optimal for him. By contrast, if he sells variant 1 to consumer 1 only, he can sell it at a price equal to 10, realizing 9 units of profits, which is the maximum over all alternatives open to the monopolist. Thus we conclude that the monopolist, when guided by the profit-maximization criterion, is not led spontaneously to select a product quality which would be optimal from the viewpoint of consumers. In the preceding example he selects a quality which is too low, compared with the social optimum. But it can also happen that the reverse arises, namely that the quality provided by the monopolist is too high, when the cost of quality is taken into account (on this point, see also Tirole 1988: 100–1).

The examples just studied correspond to the two cases of product differentiation analysed in Chapter 2, namely *horizontal* product differentiation for the first example (some consumers prefer blue cars to red ones, and vice versa for others) and *vertical* for the second one (all consumers prefer the second variant). We will now analyse duopoly competition corresponding to each of these two cases.

4.2 Duopoly and product differentiation

The neoclassical theory of the firm depicts the entrepreneur as a decision agent whose role is to select the quantities, and sometimes the prices, of the products he produces or of the factors he uses in the production process. The list of available products is given *ex ante*, and the possibility of the firm intervening in the definition of the characteristics of the products it sells is not considered. In reality, things are not so simple. In several cases, the choice of the firm also bears on which products, or on which ladder of products, to produce and to sell. We have just considered two situations of this type, either when a monopolist selects a specific quality level for his product, or when he selects a particular ladder of products, as well as the corresponding price constellation. How does this selection operate in the context of strategic interaction?

4.2.1 *Horizontal product differentiation*

The first attempt to integrate product and price selection into a context of strategic competition was made by Hotelling (1929). In this celebrated paper, Hotelling studied the problem of *spatial competition*, which corresponds to the case of horizontal product differentiation. To illustrate, consider two sellers of bottles of cola located at two points on a beach of given length, L. The beach is uniformly covered by a population of bathers who constitute the clients of the sellers. Each of these bathers will go and buy cola from one of the two stores, located respectively at a distance a from the left extremity 0 of the beach and at a distance b from the right extremity L (see Fig. 4.1). The total cost to be borne

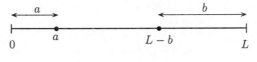

FIG. 4.1.

by a particular bather is equal to the price to be paid for the cola at the store he has selected, augmented by a *transportation cost*, denoted by $c(x)$, related to the distance x he has to walk in order to reach it. The question raised by Hotelling in this context deals simultaneously with the problem of *price determination* (the price at which each seller will decide to sell cola) and the problem of *product selection* (the pair of locations the sellers will select to set up their stores). First, it is important to stress that these two problems are intimately related: clearly, the nature of price competition between the sellers depends on the locations of their stores. If, for instance, they decide to locate at the same place, price competition will turn out to be very harsh; they would be selling a perfectly homogeneous product since nothing distinguishes the cola sold by the first seller from that sold by the second. Indeed, all consumers must in any case go to where both shops are located. But in the case of two homogeneous products, we know from Bertrand that the only non-cooperative equilibrium in price is the competitive solution! If, on the other hand, both sellers elect to locate as far as possible from each other, one at each end of the beach, price competition clearly will be considerably weakened. Due to transportation costs, a seller will have to consent to a substantial price reduction in order to convince some of his rival's customers to change their loyalties, and buy from himself rather than from the rival. Most probably, the loss due to this price reduction will not be compensated by the increase in receipts expected from the increase in market share resulting from it.

The problems of price determination and product selection being so entangled, it is necessary to treat them simultaneously. Hotelling then suggests a concept of equilibrium (*perfect equilibrium*) in which firms select their location while anticipating the nature of price competition which will follow from their selection. Three questions have to be answered about such an equilibrium. First, does there always exist an equilibrium? Second, if there does, what can be deduced concerning the locations selected at equilibrium by the firms and concerning the prices of the products? Should it be expected that firms elect at their equilibrium locations to set up their stores close to each other, thereby running the risk of a tough price competition? Or, on the other hand, will they prefer to locate far apart from each other so as to enjoy 'local monopoly' power? Finally, what are the effects of entry of new firms into the same market? Precise answers to these questions are probably too difficult to develop in the framework of this little monograph. I wish, however, to evoke the results of this analysis, and compare them to those obtained in the more traditional approach to market equilibrium.

First let us consider the problem of existence of a price equilibrium, as formulated initially by Hotelling (1929). In this formulation, Hotelling supposes that the transportation cost function $c(x)$ is a *linear increasing* function of the distance; that is, $c(x) = cx, c > 0$. Given a precise analytical expression for the transportation costs, it is easy to derive the demand at each store, given their location, as a function of the prices quoted by the two sellers, and, accordingly, their receipts as a function of the same prices. To each pair of locations, there corresponds a game, with the two sellers as players, with prices as strategies, and receipts as payoffs. An equilibrium in this game consists of a pair of prices such that no seller can increase his receipts by a unilateral deviation from the price selected at equilibrium (non-cooperative equilibrium).

Without entering into the details (the interested reader may refer to d'Aspremont *et al.* 1979), it can be shown that, with linear transportation costs, a price equilibrium exists *only if sellers' locations are sufficiently far apart from each other*. In other words, when sellers have their stores far enough apart – that is, when they sell products which are sufficiently differentiated – there exists a unique price equilibrium at which neither seller can gain any advantage by adjusting his price in the hope of increasing his profit. By contrast, when competitors are located close to each other, and sell accordingly 'too' similar products, *a price war* is unavoidable: whatever the pair of prices, at least one of the two sellers can increase his profit by deviating from it and selecting another price, undercutting the price set by his competitor at the corresponding pair. It is easy to understand this result using the following intuitive reasoning. Suppose that both sellers are located very close to each other and have selected prices such that each serves his 'hinterland' (namely, the interval $(0, a)$ for seller 1 and the interval $(L - b, L)$ for seller 2 in Fig. 4.1). Since we have assumed that the two stores are very close to each other, it should not require an important price cut by one of the sellers in order to attract all the customers of his rival, *including those who are located in his hinterland*. But then the rival has a zero market share and zero profit, so that he will also undercut the price of his competitor and corner in turn the whole market. Both prices will accordingly descend up to the point at which it will start to be advantageous to *increase* the price and serve only the hinterland at this increased price (when prices are sufficiently low, the hinterland remains faithful to its seller because the unit price cost is small compared with the transportation cost). Then prices start to cycle, preventing the existence of a price equilibrium. On the other hand, when sellers are sufficiently far apart, it is not in their interest to lower their price in order to win over the customers located in the rival hinterland: this would require such a substantial price cut that it would entail a considerable reduction in receipts.

Let us now examine how the above conclusion about price competition influences the nature of competition between sellers concerning the choice of their location. To the extent that the effects of this competition clearly depend on the ensuing price competition, the analysis of the latter serves *in fine* to evaluate the receipts of the sellers when they select the location of their store. This can be obtained by substituting, in the receipts of the sellers, the prices by their values at equilibrium in the price game. Then the receipt functions of the sellers depend only on locations, and a game, with locations as strategies, can be unambiguously defined. Unfortunately, this would require that for any pair of locations there would exist a unique price equilibrium which corresponds to it, and we have just seen that this is not the case: when sellers are not far enough apart, there exists no price equilibrium! Accordingly, the analysis of receipts as functions of locational choices is only valid in the domain of location pairs for which a price equilibrium exists. In this domain, it can be shown that the receipts of the sellers increase in proportion as they get closer and closer to each other. It was incidentally this observation which led Hotelling to state his famous *principle of minimum differentiation*, according to which sellers would spontaneously be induced to select products which are very similar. Unfortunately, this remark did not take into account the fact that, when they are too close, no price equilibrium exists. As a conclusion, it is difficult to give a completely clear answer to the second question formulated above: where the sellers will choose to locate their stores. Undoubtedly there is a tendency for the sellers to get closer to each other in the area of locations in which a price equilibrium exists, but nothing can be said when no price equilibrium exists, which is precisely the case when the sellers are getting too close to each other.

In order to clarify the answer to the question of locational choice (or, perhaps, to obscure it a little more), it is worthwhile to consider a slight variation of Hotelling's model. In this alternative version, let us assume that transportation costs are a *quadratic function* of distance, namely $c(x) = cx^2$, with x denoting the distance the consumer has to walk to the store he has decided to patronize. Performing a similar analysis to that pursued above under the assumption of linear transportation costs leads to very different conclusions. First of all, there now exists a price equilibrium corresponding to *every* pair of locations. Furthermore, and this is more significant, when these equilibrium prices are substituted in the receipt functions of the sellers, it turns out that, whatever the pair of locations considered, these receipts increase *when the sellers go farther apart from each other*. Thus we obtain here a radically different conclusion than in the case of linear tranportation costs. In the latter case, the receipts of the sellers increase when the distance between their shops diminishes, at least in the domain of locations for which a price equilibrium exists. In the former case, receipts decrease when sellers get closer to each other, and this is true in the entire domain of locations! Accordingly, under quadratic transportation costs, firms will decide to locate as far apart from each other as possible.

What can we conclude from the above? We must accept a negative conclusion concerning the question of location choice, or product selection, in the case of horizontal product differentiation: there exists no clear answer to the question whether sellers will decide to sell close, or far, product substitutes (in the spatial context, 'close' and 'far' refer to distances between locations). In the linear case, there exists an incentive to attenuate product differentiation, but this tendency creates the threat of a price war, which invalidates a 'principle of minimum product differentiation'. In the quadratic case, there is an incentive for the sellers to increase the difference between their products in order to benefit from 'local monopolies' and to relax price competition. These diametrically opposite conclusions probably reveal that, in other intermediate cases, there would exist a kind of 'equilibrium' rate of product differentiation such that no seller would benefit when altering the characteristics of his product, given the characteristics of the variant selected by his rival. In any case, *some* differentiation must exist at such an equilibrium for, otherwise, reasoning *à la* Bertrand would reveal that the sellers make zero profits while they could obtain positive profits by introducing the required product differences. These results clearly invalidate the existence of a principle of minimum differentiation. By differentiating adequately their product from the variant selected by the rival firm, each competitor is able to 'smooth' price rivalry, which is so severe when the products are perfect substitutes.

4.2.2 *Vertical product differentiation*

In order to study *vertical* product differentiation under duopoly, we consider a model in which the population of potential buyers is spread over a given range of income levels. This model is based on the idea that consumers with high income levels will want to purchase the luxury variant of the product, while the standard

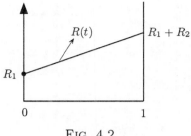

FIG. 4.2.

variant will be bought by consumers in the low-income class. Firm 1 sells the standard product at price p_1 and firm 2 the luxury variant at price p_2. All consumers are identical in terms of their preferences, but differ in income level. We represent these differences by assuming the unit interval in order of increasing income, the poorest consumer (represented by 0) owning an income R_1 and the richest (represented by 1) an income equal to $R_1 + R_2$. As for the consumers located within the unit interval, they have an intermediate income $R(t)$ defined by $R_1 + R_2 t = R(t)$ (t denoting any point in the interval). Figure 4.2 provides an illustration of the income distribution. We notice that the parameter R_1 is proportional to the average income of the population when R_2 is kept constant; similarly, the parameter R_2 is proportional to the standard deviation of the income distribution when the total mass of income is kept constant. We assume that the utility of a consumer owning an income $R(t)$ and a unit of the luxury variant (or standard variant) is equal to $u_2 R(t)$ (or $u_1 R(t)$). Finally, when the consumer does not consume either variant, his utility is given by $u_0 R(t)$. Since all consumers prefer variant 2 to variant 1, we have $u_2 > u_1$. Furthermore, since consumption of variant 1 is preferred to nothing, we also assume: $u_1 > u_0$. Notice that it is also supposed that consumers make mutually exclusive purchases: when they decide to buy a unit of one of the two variants, it is at the exclusion of the other.

From the above assumptions we may easily derive the reservation prices of consumer t for variants 1 and 2, which we denote by $\pi_1(t)$ and $\pi_2(t)$, respectively. Given that the utility obtained when buying the product must exceed the utility obtained when not buying it, consumer t is willing to buy the standard variant when the inequality: $u_1(R(t) - \pi_1(t)) > u_0 R(t)$ holds so that the reservation price for the standard variant is given by $\pi_1(t) = \frac{u_1 - u_0}{u_1} R(t)$. At that price consumer t would be indifferent between buying a unit of product 1 or keeping his income unchanged. By a similar reasoning, the luxury variant would be bought only if $u_2(R(t) - \pi_2(t)) = u_2(R_1 + R_2 t - \pi_2(t)) > u_0(R_1 + R_2 t) = u_0 R(t)$, or $\pi_2(t) = \frac{u_2 - u_0}{u_2} R(t)$. In Fig. 4.3 both $\pi_1(t)$ and $\pi_2(t)$ are represented. Now, given the prices p_1 and p_2 set by firms 1 and 2 respectively, how are consumers buying one of the two variants of the product distributed between the two firms? First of all we must notice that the set of consumers t for which both the inequalities $\pi_1(t) < p_1$ and $\pi_2(t) < p_2$ hold, buy neither of the two variants: the prices set by the sellers

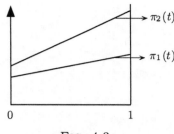

FIG. 4.3.

exceed their reservation prices. The remaining consumers buy either the first variant or the second. They select the first if and only if the utility obtained from consuming the first variant and paying the price p_1 exceeds the utility of consuming the second and paying p_2, that is, if and only if $u_1(R(t) - p_1) > u_2(R(t) - p_2)$. It can be shown that this inequality is equivalent to the condition

$$u_2\pi_2(t) - u_1\pi_1(t) < u_2 p_2 - u_1 p_1 \tag{4.1}$$

or, dividing both sides of the inequality by u_1,

$$\frac{u_2}{u_1}\pi_2(t) - \pi_1(t) < \frac{u_2}{u_1}p_2 - p_1 = \nu.$$

Three possible distributions of the consumers between the two firms are represented in Fig. 4.4 as a function of the difference $\frac{u_2}{u_1}p_2 - p_1 = \nu$. In case A, all consumers located to the left of the consumer $t(p_1)$ – the consumer indifferent between buying nothing and buying variant 1 at price p_1 – do not buy either variant since both prices exceed their reservation prices: these are the consumers located in the low-income class. The average-income class, that is, those consumers located between $t(p_1)$ and $t(p_1, p_2)$ – the latter being the consumer indifferent between buying variant 1 at price p_1 and variant 2 at price p_2 – buy

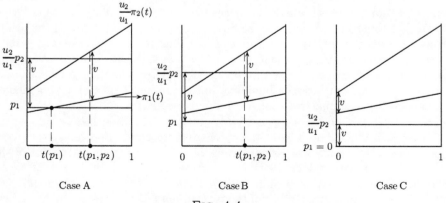

Case A   Case B   Case C

FIG. 4.4.

variant 1. Finally, the 'richest' consumers – those located between $t(p_1, p_2)$ and 1 – prefer to buy the luxury variant. The main characteristic of case A is that, at the pair of prices (p_1, p_2), the market is not 'covered': some consumers, those located between 0 and $t(p_1)$, prefer to refrain from consuming either of the two variants. By contrast, in case B, the market is covered and the consumer $t(p_1, p_2)$ separates those who buy variant 1 from those who buy variant 2. Finally, case C corresponds to a situation in which the seller of variant 1 sets a price equal to 0, and seller 2 quotes the price p_2 which makes the poorest consumer located at 0 indifferent between buying variant 1 at zero price and variant 2 at p_2. In this case, the market is 'saturated' by firm 2 which sells its variant to the whole population of consumers.

According to the cases we have just identified, three market structures can emerge under vertical product differentiation, depending on the pair of prices (p_1, p_2) selected by the rival firms. In the first, the market is not covered and some consumers would still be willing to buy the standard variant if its price diminished. In the second structure, the market is saturated, and both firms have a positive market share. Finally, corresponding to the third case, the market is fully covered by firm 2 which has succeeded in eliminating firm 1, in spite of the fact that this firm has selected a price equal to 0. Then the question arises: under which conditions will cases A, B and C be observed at the non-cooperative equilibrium in prices? The answer to this question depends of course on the values of the parameters defining our problem, namely the parameters R_1 and R_2 related to the income distribution, and the parameters u_1 and u_2 which determine how far the luxury variant 'dominates' the standard one in the tastes of the consumers. It can be shown that the non-cooperative equilibrium corresponds to case A whenever $\frac{R_1}{R_2} < \frac{u_2 - u_1}{3(u_2 - u_0)}$, to case B whenever $\frac{u_2 - u_1}{3(u_2 - u_0)} < \frac{R_1}{R_2} < 1$, and to case C when $\frac{R_1}{R_2} > 1$. Furthermore, in case B, equilibrium prices are given by $p_1^* = \frac{(u_2 - u_1)(R_2 - R_1)}{3u_1}$ and $p_2^* = \frac{(u_2 - u_1)(R_2 + R_1)}{3u_2}$; and in case C, by $p_1^* = 0$ and $p_2^* = \frac{(u_2 - u_1)R_1}{u_2}$ (the interested reader can consult Gabszewicz and Thisse 1979). Thus we obtain that, when $\frac{R_1}{R_2} < \frac{u_2 - u_1}{3(u_2 - u_0)}$, that is, for weak values of the ratio $\frac{R_1}{R_2}$, both sellers have a positive market share and the market is not fully covered. Weak values of the ratio correspond to a weak average income (R_1 small) and/or a high-income dispersion (R_2 large): only relatively rich consumers can afford to buy the standard variant, while the high-income class buys the luxury variant at a very high price. By contrast, when the ratio $\frac{R_1}{R_2}$ increases, either because the average income increases or because the dispersion of income decreases, the market becomes covered at equilibrium: even the poorest consumers can afford to buy the standard variant. Finally, when the ratio $\frac{R_1}{R_2}$ exceeds 1, which corresponds to a weak dispersion and/or a high average income, all consumers decide to buy the luxury variant at equilibrium.

It is useful to discuss the above results in terms of entry. Suppose, indeed, that firm 1 initially occupies the market with the standard product and benefits from a monopoly position; firm 2 selling the higher-quality product enters the market.

When $\frac{R_1}{R_2} < 1$ (case A or B), this entry is compatible with the persistence of the standard product at equilibrium after entry. By contrast, as soon as $\frac{R_1}{R_2} > 1$ (case C), the entry of a higher-quality product must necessarily be accompanied by the exit of the pre-existing product. Furthermore, at the resulting equilibrium, the equilibrium price p_2^* is the highest price that firm 2 can set while guaranteeing that firm 1, even when quoting a zero price, cannot remain in the market with a positive market share (see Fig. 4.4, case C). The price p_2^* plays a role which is analogous to that played by the limit price in limit pricing theory. As in this theory, it can easily be checked that the price p_2^* is always smaller than the monopoly price which would have been announced by firm 2 in the absence of potential competition from firm 1.

Now let us consider the problem of quality selection . Suppose that firm 2 contemplates the possibility of entry and controls the value of the parameter u_2: the higher u_2, the higher the quality of the product sold by the firm. The question is whether it is more advantageous for the entrant to select a quality which is close to the quality of the existing product, with a view to possibly capturing the customers of the incumbent firm, or to differentiate the product, so as to benefit from a 'local monopoly' position. We again find the question posed by Hotelling, but formulated now in the context of vertical product differentiation. When $\frac{R_1}{R_2} > 1$ (case A), we get an immediate answer: firm 2 enters the market, serves the whole market at the equilibrium price $p_2^* = \frac{(u_2 - u_1)R_1}{u_2}$ and, since this price, as well as receipts, are increasing functions of u_2, firm 2 selects the highest possible value for it, that is, firm 2 selects the highest possible quality. Now consider the case $\frac{R_1}{R_2} < 1$ (case B or C). If firm 2 decides to enter with a variant which is close to the variant of the incumbent firm, the quality differential $u_2 - u_1$ tends to zero and the two equilibrium prices $p_1^* = \frac{(u_2 - u_1)(R_2 - R_1)}{3u_1}$ and $p_2^* = \frac{(u_2 - u_1)(2R_2 + R_1)}{3u_2}$ also tend simultaneously to zero. This is not surprising: when u_2 tends to u_1, both products tend to become perfect substitutes and Bertrand equilibrium analysis applies: both prices tend to zero, which is the competitive price in the homogeneous case. Again, firm 2 benefits from selecting the highest possible quality, thereby maximizing product differentiation with a view to relaxing price competition with the incumbent firm. Hotelling's conjecture about the existence of a principle of minimal differentiation is invalidated in the case of vertical product differentiation as well. When emphasizing the quality differential between their variants, firms protect themselves against the risk of running into a price war, which is inherent to situations in which they sell almost homogeneous products.

4.3   Entry in a differentiated market

The two preceding sections have been devoted to the study of a differentiated market with a small number of competitors. If there are no barriers to entry, it is natural to examine the effects of entry on a market in which the firms sell products which, although not homogeneous, are close substitutes for the variants already sold by the incumbent firms. In particular, we must examine whether entry with substitute products has the same consequences as those observed when entry takes place with a strictly homogeneous product. Chamberlin (1933) was the first economist to analyse entry with differentiated products. He started from the observation that there are numerous markets on which firms, far from selling a homogeneous product, compete with variants which are, however, close substitutes. Furthermore, he noticed that this situation is often realized in a market consisting of a large number of firms, each selling a different variant. A good example corresponding to this market structure is the case of grocery stores in a large city: there are many such stores in the city, but each sells a differentiated product since it is located in a specific spatial environment.

Without going into a rigorous analysis, Chamberlin then developed the following argument. Since products are differentiated, each competitor is aware that the demand for his product depends on the price he decides to quote. Nevertheless, due to the existence of a large number of sellers, none of them is aware that demand for his own product also depends on the prices set by his competitors. Each seller then behaves as a monopolist on his own individual market. However, when new firms penetrate the market, they progressively capture the customers of the incumbent firms, thereby reducing the demand on each of them: at each price, incumbents' demand is smaller and more elastic than before entry. Beyond some number of entrants, it will no longer be possible for any firm to sell a positive quantity of output at a price which could cover its average cost of production: each existing firm in the industry makes zero profit and further entry is henceforth impossible.

Figure 4.5 represents the long-run industry equilibrium corresponding to this situation. The individual firm produces a quantity Q_{CM} and sells it at price p_{CM}, given its demand function DD' obtained as a result of entry of other firms selling substitute products in the industry. In Fig. 4.5 we notice that the quan-

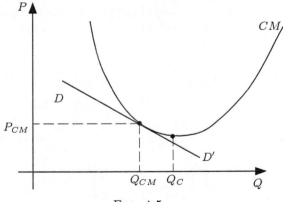

FIG. 4.5.

tity Q_{CM} sold at the long-run equilibrium is smaller than the quantity Q_C which minimizes the average cost function M_C, and which is also the quantity which would have been produced by the firm if entry had taken place on a purely competitive market. Remember indeed that entry in a competitive industry with a homogeneous product drives each firm's output to the level at which its average cost is minimal (see Section 2.1.1). By contrast, *at the long-run equilibrium in a differentiated industry, each firm produces a level of output which is smaller than its capacity* (we have already noticed the existence of this excess capacity property at the long-run equilibrium obtained under strategic entry with a homogeneous product).

4.3.1 *Entry under horizontal product differentiation*

As already noted in Chapter 2, the two assumptions underlying Chamberlinian analysis – the seller's perception of price dependence on quantity and, simultaneously, his ignorance of strategic interaction – seem hardly compatible. In the same chapter we explained at length how localized competition creates a chain structure of demand, implying that each firm competes directly only with the firms which are its immediate neighbours in the space of characteristics, and not with the whole population of firms operating in the industry. As a consequence, when a firm perceives that the quantity it sells depends on the price it quotes, it should also perceive the strategic interaction existing between the few sellers which are its immediate neighbours. Let us illustrate this with the following very simple model describing strategic entry on a circular market. This covers the case of entry under horizontal differentiation. The space of characteristics is represented by a circle of unit circumference. Consumers are uniformly distributed on the circle and the firms (products), n in number, are equally spaced around the same circle, as in Fig. 4.6. Let us assume that transportation cost is a quadratic function of distance, $c(x) = tx^2$, with x denoting the distance. The first step in our reasoning consists of identifying the demand addressed to a particular firm i as a function of its own price p_i and of the prices of its neighbours, firms $i-1$ and $i+1$. For a particular pair of prices p_{i-1} and p_{i+1}, demand D_i on firm i

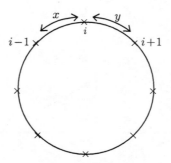

FIG. 4.6.

can be determined in the following manner. Between i and $i-1$, consumers are shared between the two firms. Among them, there exists a consumer who is just indifferent between buying from either of these firms. For this consumer, the price p_i augmented by the transportation cost tx^2 to be paid to buy from firm i must necessarily be equal to the price p_{i-1} augmented by the transportation cost $t(\frac{1}{n} - x)^2$ to be paid to buy from firm $i-1$ (notice that we use the property that all firms are located at equal distance $\frac{1}{n}$ from each other). From the equality

$$tx^2 + pi = t\left(\frac{1}{n} - x\right)^2 + p_{i-1},$$

we obtain

$$x = \frac{p_{i-1} - p_i}{2t/n} + \frac{1}{2n}.$$

All consumers located between firm i and the point located upwards of i at a distance x of it patronize firm i. An analogous reasoning enables us to identify the consumer located between firm i and firm $i+1$ who is just indifferent between buying from firm i at price p_i and buying from firm $i+1$ at price p_{i+1}, namely

$$y = \frac{p_{i+1} - p_i}{2t/n} + \frac{1}{2n}.$$

The demand D_i on firm i then obtains by adding the market shares lying on both sides of its position on the circle, $x + y$, or

$$D_i(p_{i-1}, pi, p_{i+1}) = \frac{p_{i-1} - 2p_i + p_{i+1}}{2t/n} + \frac{1}{n}.$$

This expression clearly reveals that demand on firm i does not depend on price strategies selected by firms which are not immediate neighbours of it. By contrast, it depends on the prices selected by its two neighboring firms in the space of characteristics (here the circle). This property constitutes the very essence of localized competition. As expected, demand D_i decreases with p_i, while it increases with p_{i-1} and p_{i+1}: the differentiated variants are indeed product substitutes. If the marginal production cost c is constant and identical for all firms, the profit of firm i is given by

$$\pi_i(p_{i-1}, p_i, p_{i+1}) = (p_i - c)D_i(p_{i-1}, p_i, p_{i+1}).$$

Due to the symmetry of the model, it must be expected that all firms select the same price, say p^*, at the non-cooperative price equilibrium. First-order conditions imply that this is indeed the case, with $p^* = c + \frac{t}{n^2}$.

First we notice that, due to the fact that products are differentiated, each firm has the possibility of selling its product at a price which exceeds its marginal cost c. While price competition between two firms is already sufficient to erode the total amount of profits in the industry when firms sell a homogeneous product, horizontal product differentiation endows firms with 'local monopoly' power, leading to strictly positive profit margins at equilibrium. This is true even if strategies are not quantities but prices. The higher the unit transportation cost t, the stronger the monopoly power. This reflects the fact that this cost measures the disutility for the consumer to buy from a shop which is remote from the one which is the closest to him. The higher t, the more difficult for the former to compete with the latter, and the farther the equilibrium price p^* from the marginal cost c. On the other hand, notice that the equilibrium price p^* tends to the competitive price c when the number n of firms tends to infinity. Finally, in the absence of set-up costs, entry in a horizontally differentiated market is never impossible: whatever the number of incumbent firms, there is always room for new firms. By contrast, the existence of a fixed cost will necessarily limit the number of firms: with free entry into the industry, the number of firms cannot increase beyond the point at which the receipts of each firm drop below its fixed cost of production. The lower this fixed cost, the higher the number of firms at long-run equilibrium.

In the above analysis we have implicitly assumed that firms enter the industry simultaneously. We could have assumed as well that firms enter sequentially without having the possibility of changing, after entry, the location they have selected. The equilibrium analysis must then take into account how the existing firms anticipate which locations will be selected by later entrants. In the case of sequential entry, it can be shown that profits remain strictly positive at the long-run equilibrium, even with free entry (see, on this topic, Eaton and Lipsey 1980).

4.3.2 *Entry under vertical product differentiation*

Now let us consider entry when it takes place in a *vertically* differentiated industry. To simplify, we shall assume that the entrant always supplies a variant which is of a higher quality than those already supplied by incumbent firms. This assumption is not unreasonable since it reflects the fact that new variants generally incorporate some technical improvement from which earlier variants have not benefited. The analysis provided above for the duopoly case can then be extended to a vertically differentiated oligopoly including n firms, ranked in order of increasing quality, the 'quality' parameter u_k of firm k being larger than the quality parameter u_{k-1} of firm $k - 1$, for all $k = 1, \ldots, n$. Now imagine the entry of an $(n + 1)$th product with a quality u_{n+1} which exceeds the quality u_n.

At the new equilibrium prevailing after entry, two situations may be observed. In the first, there are still some consumers who do not buy either of the variants offered by the industry after entry. This corresponds to case A identified above, when firm 1 was the only one present in the industry before the entry of firm 2, but when, after the entry of the latter, there were still some consumers who did not buy either variant 1 or variant 2 at the new price equilibrium. In the second situation, the market is covered after the entry of firm $n+1$: all consumers decide to buy one of the two variants. This corresponds to cases B and C identified above. But, as in these cases, we must distinguish between two possibilities. In the first, all firms obtain a strictly positive market share at the new price equilibrium prevailing after entry: this is case B. In the second situation, *the entry of the $(n+1)$th firm generates a new price equilibrium at which the lowest-quality firm, even setting a zero price, is excluded from the industry, and is replaced by firm $n+1$ which sells the highest quality among all firms in the industry*: this is case C. In this case, the market is too 'narrow' to allow more than n firms to coexist at equilibrium: entry of a higher-quality variant is necessarily accompanied by the exit of the existing variant of lowest quality. In fact, this result simply generalizes a property we have already observed in duopoly when $\frac{R_1}{R_2}$ is larger than 1; under this assumption, firm 2 excludes firm 1 from the market. It can be shown that, whatever the value of the ratio $\frac{R_1}{R_2}$, that is, whatever the value of the average income and income dispersion, there always exists an upper bound on the number of products which can coexist in the industry. Furthermore, this number is an increasing function of income dispersion.

We have stated the above properties assuming implicitly that all variants are produced at zero costs. This is not a realistic assumption, to the extent that production costs most probably increase with product quality. However, it can be shown that these properties remain valid when production costs do not increase 'too' much with quality. In this case, only those firms whose cost–quality ratio is the lowest are able to survive at equilibrium (see Shaked and Sutton (1983)).

In conclusion, entry into a vertically differentiated industry leads to a long-run market structure which considerably differs from the long-run equilibrium observed when products are differentiated horizontally, or are not differentiated at all. In the latter cases, in the absence of fixed costs or significant entry barriers, a large number of firms should be expected at the long-run industry equilibrium so that it does not seem unrealistic to predict a price-taking behaviour for the sellers operating in such environments. By contrast, entry into a vertically differentiated industry generates a natural oligopoly structure: according to the extent of income dispersion in the population, the industry will be more or less rapidly saturated, leaving room at equilibrium for a restricted number of firms only. In this case, it should be expected that the surviving firms are aware of their strategic interaction, and thus select their price and quality using explicitly their strategic position: the competitive assumption is certainly less credible in this context.

The intuition behind the above result is simple to understand. If consumers do not differ very much from each other in their tastes and income, the surplus that a firm can obtain by selling the highest-quality variant at a price which would induce the poorest consumer to buy it is not very substantial. By contrast, if income is very much dispersed throughout the population, the surplus obtained by the richest consumers and which can be captured by the firm selling the highest quality does not justify a price decrease sufficient to attract consumers with a lower income. Then room is left for the entry of a more standardized variant which is to be sold to these less rich consumers. But the survival of one or several further variants, of still lower quality, would require more and more significant disparities of income in the population. Paradoxically, the more egalitarian the income distribution, the smaller the number of firms which may coexist at equilibrium, and the weaker the competition in the industry!

Among the assumptions underlying the competitive paradigm, product homogeneity guarantees that no seller can set a price which would exceed the 'market' price. Otherwise all consumers considering the products sold by competitors as identical would certainly prefer to buy from them. We have studied in this chapter how relaxing this assumption can affect the nature of competition among firms. We have still to examine how this competition is affected when the assumption of perfect information of consumers about price or quality is in turn abandoned. This is the object of the next chapter.

5

IMPERFECT INFORMATION

We study in this chapter some aspects of the role played by imperfect information held by consumers on the nature of competition among firms. As observed in our introduction, this represents a broad topic dealing with the fundamental question of price formation. We shall limit ourselves to two illustrations: the first deals with imperfect information about *prices* (Section 5.1) and the second about *quality* (Section 5.2).

5.1   Imperfect information about prices

Two major remarks were formulated in Chapter 2 concerning imperfect information held by consumers about the prices set by firms operating in a particular industry. First, some *inertia* is observed in the search process through which consumers try to improve their information about existing prices: this inertia is caused by the costs involved in this process. On the other hand, firms exploit this inertia by manipulating their prices in order to create incentives which slow down the search process of consumers. Among the various problems related to imperfect information about prices evoked in Chapter 2, we have chosen to illustrate particularly how rival firms manipulate their prices in order to exploit consumers' inertia with regard to search. Since the spatial dispersion of sellers constitutes a major reason why consumers do not hold full information about selling prices, we have formulated this illustration in the context of spatial competition, in which consumers' inertia is essentially related to information costs to be incurred due precisely to sellers' spatial dispersion.

The model we propose to analyse is, again, a variant of the duopoly spatial competition model of Hotelling considered in Section 4.2.1. Contrary to Hotelling's assumption that consumers have full information on both prices, we suppose now that they know *only the price set by the seller who is located closer to them, but not the price set by the seller located farther from them.*

Consider two merchants, 1 and 2, located, respectively, at points a and $L - b$ of a linear market $(0, L)$. Consumers are uniformly distributed along the same interval (see Fig. 5.1). Suppose further that all consumers located closer to seller

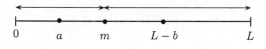

FIG. 5.1.

1 than seller 2 (the interval $A_1 = [0, m]$) know the price p_1 set by seller 1, but
not the price p_2 announced by seller 2 (the point m is located mid-way between
points a and $L - b$ and is thus equal to $\frac{L+a-b}{2}$). Similarly consumers located in
the interval $A_2 = [m, L]$ know p_2, but not p_1. We call the interval A_1 (or A_2)
the natural market of firm 1 (or firm 2). Finally, we assume that consumers can
obtain full information about the price they do not know at a cost which increases
with the distance which separates them from the corresponding firm (this would
be the case, for instance, if the information is obtained by calling the firm whose
price is not known). Assuming that firms know that their consumers do not
have full knowledge of prices, how could they exploit it at the non-cooperative
equilibrium in prices (p_1^*, p_2^*)? This is an interesting question in particular because
it will allow us to compare the answer we obtain from Hotelling's model where
consumers are assumed to enjoy full information on prices. To examine this
question, it is useful to refer to Fig. 5.2. Here $p_1(t)$ denotes the highest price

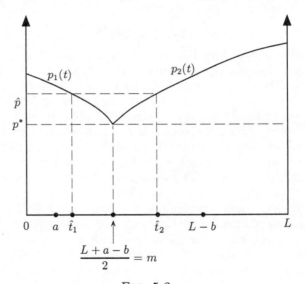

FIG. 5.2.

of firm 1 which consumer t, located in the natural market of seller 1, would be
willing to tolerate without trying to find out the price p_2. The function $p_2(t)$
is defined analogously for a consumer t located in the natural market A_2 of
seller 2. In both cases, when the known price exceeds the 'tolerated' price, the
consumer prefers to pay the information cost so as to obtain full information
on the price set by the competitor (we shall see further how the functions $p_1(t)$
and $p_2(t)$ can be explicitly derived from beliefs of the consumers about the value
of the unknown price). The fact that these functions decrease in proportion as
we consider consumers located closer and closer to the consumer $m = \frac{L+a-b}{2}$
located at the border between the natural markets, comes from the assumption

that information costs increase with distance. The farther away a consumer is located from the shop whose price he does not know, the higher the price he would be willing to tolerate at the shop whose price he knows.

Let us show that the only possible candidate as a non-cooperative equilibrium is the pair of prices at which each firm sets the same price $p^* = p_1(m)$, namely the price which makes the consumer at the borderline between the two natural markets indifferent between trying to find out the price he does not know and buying at the one he knows.

First notice that no pair of prices at which one of the sellers would announce a price strictly lower than p^* could be an equilibrium: this seller could increase his price while keeping his natural market, which would entail an increase in receipts, contradicting the fact that this pair is a non-cooperative equilibrium. Furthermore, it is clear that the sellers must necessarily announce the same price, for, otherwise, the firm announcing the lowest price could increase his price without losing any customers. This comes from the fact that, if both firms announce a price which exceeds p^*, and these differ from each other, the set of consumers who proceed to search will necessarily buy from the seller announcing the lowest price since all of them have full information on prices. This seller can then increase his price without losing these customers, thereby increasing his receipts. Consequently, a situation where the sellers announce different prices cannot be an equilibrium. Finally, it remains to exclude, as a possible equilibrium, any pair of prices where both firms would announce the same price, say $\hat{p}$, with $\hat{p} > p^*$. Using Fig. 5.2, we see that all consumers in the interval $(\hat{t}_1, \hat{t}_2)$ try to obtain information about the price of the competitor located farther from them. Each seller can thus capture all these customers by lowering his price slightly below $\hat{p}$, and thereby increasing his receipts, a contradiction. Consequently, it follows from the above reasoning that the only pair of prices which could be a non-cooperative equilibrium is (p^*, p^*) .

First of all, it is remarkable that, at this pair of prices, no consumer is searching for information about the price announced by the seller whose price he does not know: the price p^* is the highest price which can be set by a seller while guaranteeing that all consumers in his natural market will continue to buy from him. The intuition underlying this result is easy to capture. If a firm announces a price which exceeds p^*, it creates incentives for some customers in its natural market, those located the closest to its competitor, to try to find out the price of the latter. Since these consumers will indeed know that the price of the latter is lower, it is better to keep p^* in order to prevent this search. This confirms that firms manipulate prices so as to exploit consumers' inertia.

Notice also that the above analysis does not guarantee that the pair (p^*, p^*) is a non-cooperative equilibrium; it guarantees simply that if there exists a non-cooperative equilibrium, it must be the pair (p^*, p^*). It is thus interesting to study when this pair of prices is indeed an equilibrium, or when, for all pairs of prices, there always exists at least one seller who can deviate from the price p^* to his own advantage, in which case there would exist no equilibrium. To perform this analysis, let us first suppose that each consumer has the same beliefs concerning the unknown price set by the firm which is farther away from him, namely, a probability distribution which is uniform on a given interval of prices. Suppose also that the cost of information is, like the transportation cost in Hotelling's model, *linear* with respect to distance. Under these two assumptions, we can explicitly derive both the functions $p_1(t)$ and $p_2(t)$ and the pair of prices (p^*, p^*) constituting the only possible candidate price equilibrium (the interested reader may refer to Gabszewicz and Garella 1986). It can then be shown that this pair of prices is a non-cooperative equilibrium if and only if the two inequalities $b + 3a < L$ and $a + 3b < L$ are simultaneously satisfied. These inequalities guarantee that firms are sufficiently far apart. Furthermore, in the domain of values for a and $L - b$ in which these inequalities are satisfied, the receipts of the sellers increase when they get closer to each other.

It is interesting to compare these results with those obtained by Hotelling in the case of spatial competition with consumers *perfectly* informed about prices. We have seen in Section 4.2, that with linear transportation costs there exists a non-cooperative equilibrium only when firms are sufficiently far apart from each other. Accordingly, for both perfect and imperfect information, conditions related to the distance between firms are needed to guarantee existence of an equilibrium. However, even if these conditions are similar, the reasons why an equilibrium may not exist are very different in the two situations. In Hotelling's case, the equilibrium is destroyed when firms are too close to each other because proximity creates incentives to undercut one's competitor in order to capture its customers: a price war is brought about by insufficient product differentiation. In the case of imperfect information, no equilibrium exists when firms are too close to each other because the market between them is so narrow that no firm can justify lowering its price in order to retain its share of the natural market located between it and its competitor. Then, it is more profitable to select a high price and serve at that price only those customers located so far from one's competitor that even at that price they will not be willing to search. Of course, those consumers who are closer to the rival firm will prefer to buy from it; but the loss incurred is smaller than the benefit obtained from keeping a high price. Of course the use of this strategy prevents the pair (p^*, p^*) from being an equilibrium. *It is only when p^* corresponds for each firm to the monopoly price on its natural market that this pair is also a non-cooperative equilibrium.* By contrast, in the domain of values of a and b for which a price equilibrium exists, sellers' receipts increase when they get closer to each other, thereby creating incentives to enter the domain of values in which an equilibrium no longer exists.

We have assumed in the above analysis that consumers were themselves proceeding to the information search required by their imperfect knowledge of market prices. The opposite case of this analysis consists in assuming that firms themselves inform consumers about their existence and the price they have selected. This is the case, for instance, when firms send advertising to their customers specifying the price at which they sell their product. To model this situation, we assume that firm 1 has chosen to inform a segment of length x in the natural market of firm 2 and firm 2 a segment of length y in the natural market of firm 1.

Figure 5.3 represents the information structure of consumers when firm 1 has elected to inform a segment $(m_1, m_1 + x)$ in the natural market of firm 2 and firm 2 a segment $(m_1 - y, m_1)$ in the natural market of firm 1, with $m_1 = \frac{L + a - b}{2}$. All consumers included in the interval $(m_1 - x, m_1 + x)$ accordingly have full information on both prices, while those located to the left of m_1 only know the existence and the price of firm 1 and those located to the right of $m_1 + x$ the existence and the price of firm 2. Finally, we assume that the reservation price of the consumers for the product is equal to ν. What is the price equilibrium resulting from this structure? Consider for instance firm 1, assuming that firm

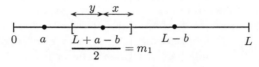

FIG. 5.3.

2 has set a price equal to p_2. If firm 1 announces a price p_1 less than p_2, all customers to the left of $m_1 + x$ buy from this firm, those to the left of $m_1 - x$ because in any case they do not know the existence of firm 2, and those between $m_1 - x$ and $m_1 + x$ because they know that firm 1 has a lower price than firm 2. By contrast, if firm 1 sets a price strictly higher than firm 2, it serves only the segment $(0, m_1 - y)$ in this firm's natural market. We assume that when both firms announce the same price, each serves its entire natural market. First, if there exists a price equilibrium (p_1^*, p_2^*), it is necessary that $p_1^* = p_2^*$. If this were not the case and we observed, for instance, $p_1^* < p_2^*$, firm 1 could increase its price without losing a customer as long as the increase remained smaller than the difference $p_2^* - p_1^*$. But then firm 1 could increase its receipts, contradicting the fact that (p_1^*, p_2^*) is an equilibrium. Thus both prices have to be equal at equilibrium, say, equal to p^*; at this price each firm serves its natural market. But this also cannot be a price equilibrium if $p^* > 0$, for each firm, by lowering slightly its price from the level p^*, would obtain as customers all those who have been informed by it in the natural market of its competitor; this would increase receipts and destroy (p^*, p^*) as a price equilibrium. It remains to consider the case when both firms announce a price equal to zero, and realize zero receipts. This cannot be an equilibrium either, since each firm would realize strictly positive receipts if it chose any price smaller than the reservation price ν and served the uninformed segment of its natural market at that price. Consequently, we must conclude that there exists no price equilibrium when firms have the possibility of informing the natural market of their rival, but do not inform all customers of this natural market.

What about when each firm informs the *whole* natural market of its rival?

Then all consumers are fully informed about both prices and the only price equilibrium is necessarily that predicted by Bertrand at which both firms announce a zero price and make zero profit. Thus we may conclude that when firms decide to distribute information about prices, either no equilibrium exists, in the case where they do not inform all the rival's customers, or they restore Bertrand competition, in the case where the rival's entire natural market is informed. On the other hand, when the firms decide to refrain from informing the clients in the natural market of the competitor, they may behave as a monopolist on their own natural market and set the price equal to ν, which allows each firm to capture the whole surplus in its market! Even in the simplified framework of our model, we are accordingly led to a similar conclusion as in the case where consumers were themselves collecting information: *when consumers are imperfectly informed about prices, firms will naturally use strategies which aim at preventing any increase in the information available to these consumers.* To this end, firms decrease their price to reinforce the natural inertia of consumers to search for a lower price, or, when this opportunity exists, they refrain from informing the customers of their rival about their own price in order to avoid the risk of a price war.

5.2   Imperfect information about quality

In order to illustrate the strategic behaviour of firms facing imperfect information held by consumers about quality, we shall limit ourselves to studying the consequences, on the prices announced at equilibrium by these firms, of a priori beliefs of consumers about the distribution of quality among firms. There are several situations in which consumers are unable to identify with certainty the quality of the products offered by different firms. Consider for instance a commercial traveller arriving in a town never visited before. This traveller may know that, of the two seafood restaurants in the town, one is selling fresh seafood while the other serves rotten fish! However, he is unable to identify a priori which restaurant offers which quality. Similarly, when quality of a product is defined by reference to its probability of failure, as with light bulbs, consumers may identify the various probabilities of failure corresponding to the products offered in the industry, without being able, however, to attribute a specific probability to each particular firm. Finally, new products are often imitated and it may be difficult for the consumers to identify the 'true' product from the fake.

In all such situations, consumers have to form their own opinion about the likelihood of events which can influence their choice. All consumers are not identical in this respect. First, the likelihood of an event can be considered a subjective matter. Furthermore, consumers do not share generally the same amount of information, either because some of them have benefited from rumours which were not available to others, or because some have already experienced one or another variant of the product available in the industry. This multiplicity of opinions leads in each specific case to a particular dispersion of beliefs among the population about the fact that any particular firm sells a variant of the product of high or low quality. When the dispersion of beliefs in the population is biased in favour of a particular firm at the expense of another, the former is said to enjoy a 'good' reputation and the latter a 'bad' one, even if this judgement does not necessarily reflect the 'objective' differential between qualities. How these a priori reputations influence price strategies of firms is now analysed.

Consider a market in which two firms compete by selling a variant of different quality. Firm 1 is assumed to sell the low-quality variant, which gives the consumer a utility level equal to u_B, while firm 2 sells the high-quality variant leading to a utility level u_A; we have of course $u_A > u_B$ (vertical product differentiation). To represent a priori beliefs of the population, let $\alpha \in [0, 1]$ represent the probability which a particular consumer assigns to the fact that the 'good' variant will be sold by firm 1 (which, remember, is not the case). When α is equal to 1, the consumer is completely erroneous. When α is equal to 0, the consumer is perfectly correct. Finally, when α takes some other value, then the closer this value is to zero, the closer it is to the truth. Now suppose that the set of values for α existing in the population is given by the interval $(\underline{\alpha}, \overline{\alpha})$. When this interval is located in the $(0, 1)$ interval in an area which is close to 1 (for instance, when $\underline{\alpha} = \frac{1}{2}$ and $\overline{\alpha} = \frac{3}{4}$), the bias of beliefs is in favour of firm 1, although it does not merit it. If, on the other hand, this interval is located close to 0 (for instance, when $\underline{\alpha} = \frac{1}{4}$ and $\overline{\alpha} = \frac{1}{2}$), then it is firm 2 which has the good reputation, on average, among the population. When the interval is located symmetrically around $\frac{1}{2}$, then there is no bias in the beliefs of the population and both firms are equally well regarded, on average.

To identify the demand on each firm as a function of their prices p^1 and p^2, we must find the consumer whose a priori belief α is such that he is indifferent between buying from firm 1 and firm 2 at these prices. Assuming that consumers maximize their expected utility, this consumer is characterized by the value of α such that $\alpha u_A + (1 - \alpha)u_B - p_1 = \alpha u_B + (1 - \alpha)u_A - p_2$: all consumers with beliefs smaller than this value buy from firm 2, and those with beliefs exceeding this value buy from firm 1. This defines the value of the demand function for each firm at the pair of prices (p_1, p_2), and we can then proceed to the determination of the price equilibrium corresponding to the domain of beliefs $(\underline{\alpha}, \overline{\alpha})$ (for more details the interested reader may refer to Gabszewicz and Grilo 1993).

What conclusions can be derived from this analysis? First, it can be shown that there always exists a unique non-cooperative price equilibrium corresponding to each domain of beliefs included in the $(0, 1)$ interval. At this equilibrium and according to the values of the extremities $\underline{\alpha}$ and $\overline{\alpha}$ of the beliefs' interval, either both firms enjoy positive market shares, or the firm benefiting from the 'good' reputation bias excludes its rival from the market and remains the only one to serve the customers. In any case, the firm with the better reputation always quotes a higher price at equilibrium. When the low-quality firm is thrown out of the market, it sets a zero price, and the firm with the good reputation quotes the highest price which is compatible with the fact of keeping the low-quality one out of the industry. We recognize again the limit pricing policy which aims in this case at excluding the firm suffering from a lower reputation in terms of the quality served.

It is also possible to examine how equilibrium prices vary with respect to the 'average' belief in the population and to the dispersion of these beliefs. In particular, it can be shown that, while keeping the average belief constant, an increase in the dispersion of beliefs must necessarily increase both prices at equilibrium. Furthermore, it is better, from the viewpoint of the consumers, that there exists some dispersion of their beliefs. If there were no dispersion at all, then all consumers would assign to each firm the same probability of selling the high-quality product. Clearly, the firm which has been assigned the higher probability, being regarded by all consumers as the high-quality one, will be able to exclude its rival from the market and quote a very high price, at the expense of consumers' welfare. However, when beliefs are positively dispersed, there exist some consumers which assign some probability to the other firm being the high-quality producer, thereby allowing the latter to compete more credibly with the former.

A further interesting point concerning the above approach is that it permits us to examine how the price equilibrium is affected by an information campaign by firm 2 about the quality of its product. Suppose, indeed, that a given fraction of the population is informed about the fact that the high-quality variant is sold by firm 2. This can be realized by distributing a sample at random to the corresponding fraction of the population, which reveals without any ambiguity that the high-quality variant is that sold by firm 2. After this distribution has been performed, the initial domain of beliefs is modified because the belief $\underline{\alpha}$ becomes henceforth equal to zero (the probability that the good variant is variant sold by firm 1) for the whole mass of consumers who have received the sample and are accordingly informed. This new domain of beliefs generates a new price equilibrium, and the comparison between this equilibrium and the one prevailing before the information campaign allows the variation in equilibrium prices resulting from it to be measured as a function of the size of the population which has been informed. This leads to the following conclusions (see Gabszewicz and Grilo 1992). First of all, if the fraction of informed population becomes too significant, the price equilibrium ceases to exist, although it always existed when no consumer held full information. The intuitive reason for this conclusion is as follows. When the mass of consumers who are informed is large, it creates an incentive for the firm selling the low-quality variant to undercut the price of firm 2, in order to capture this entire set of customers. To do so, firm 1 must indeed set a very low price since all these customers perfectly know that it sells the low-quality variant. But the receipts realized on the size of market share justify this sacrifice. This generates a price cycle preventing stabilization at an equilibrium. On the other hand, whenever an equilibrium exists, both firms have a positive market share at equilibrium. This may seem surprising to the extent that, when the whole market is informed, firm 2 excludes firm 1 by announcing a price equal to the quality differential $u_A - u_B$, which guarantees that firm 1 cannot obtain a positive market share even when quoting a zero price.

Finally, it should be noted that, in the domain where a price equilibrium exists, both prices increase at equilibrium when the mass of informed consumers increases. This may seem surprising at first sight, at least for the firm selling the low-quality product; more and more consumers are informed of this fact and, in spite of this, its receipts increase! This can be understood, however, since the increase of information provides the high-quality firm with a larger captive market, allowing firm 2 to be less agressive with respect to firm 1 and to set its price at a progressively higher level. This in turn leads firm 1 to quote a price which increases at equilibrium with the fraction of the population which is informed.

The above insights constitute only two very particular illustrations of the role played by imperfect information on the strategic behaviour of firms. This area of research is presently very active and we have not presented a complete picture of work carried out during the last decade. In particular, we have not considered investigations related to the role of *asymmetric* information of economic agents. The interested reader will find an elaborate presentation of this topic in Stiglitz (1989).

6

IMPERFECT COMPETITION AND GENERAL EQUILIBRIUM

In the previous chapters, we have considered an isolated industry with buyers behaving as price-takers, and sellers taking into account the interactive decision context in which they operate. In several respects, the present analysis differs radically from the previous approach. First, we shall now consider the process of exchange taking place simultaneously on several markets. Due to the possible substitutions and complementarities existing among the products in the preferences of the consumers, markets are interrelated: the quantity of a good desired by consumers depends on the quantities of several other goods which can be obtained through exchange. Second, we leave temporarily an analysis based on the mechanism of exchange through prices, in favour of an analysis of exchange based on the *barter* mechanism, which relies on the direct exchange of goods for goods. Finally, we also abandon the assumption according to which some agents behave as price-takers while others act strategically . We shall henceforth assume that *all* economic agents who participate in exchange adopt the same *cooperative* behaviour.

6.1 The cooperative approach

6.1.1 *The core of an exchange economy*

Barter exchange between two persons is the simplest example of an exchange process based on the principle of cooperation. Each agent initially owns some quantities of the goods, and wants to improve his position through trade with another agent. Edgeworth (1881) has specifically studied this problem in the *bilateral monopoly* model with two traders, each owning initially the total amount of a particular commodity. Consumer 1 initially owns an amount a of good 1 while consumer 2 an amount b of good 2. After exchanging the quantities x and y, the first consumer has the commodity bundle $(a - x, y)$ and the second $(x, b - y)$. In Fig. 6.1, the length of the edges of the so-called Edgeworth box represents the total quantities a and b of the two goods available in the economy. A particular point in the box represents an allocation of the two goods between the two agents. If, for instance, the allocation is given by point M, the quantities obtained by agent 1 are measured by the coordinates of M, using 0 as origin, while those obtained by agent 2 are measured by the coordinates of M using $0'$ as origin. Indifference curves of both consumers between goods are also depicted in the box. Those turning their concavity to 0 ($0'$) belong to agent 1 (agent 2). Each point in the box thus corresponds to a particular reallocation of the initial endowments between the two consumers.

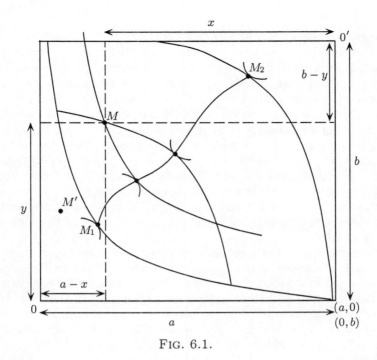

FIG. 6.1.

The question raised by Edgeworth can then be formulated as follows. What allocations should be expected as a result of barter exchange between the two traders? As we shall see, two 'reasonable' assumptions are sufficient to limit this set of allocations to the locus of points where the indifference curves of the agents are at a tangent.

The first assumption deals with individual requirements. Each agent is assumed to require to end up, after exchange, with a commodity bundle which is preferred to his initial endowment: the position of each trader must be improved through trade. In other words, none of them makes a 'present' to his counterpart. The second assumption introduces a kind of cooperation between the two parties. It asserts that an allocation will be rejected by both participants as a possible exchange arrangement when there exists another allocation at which each of them obtains a bundle which is preferred to the one he would get at that arrangement.

As a consequence of the first assumption, any allocation which would locate a trader on an indifference curve which is lower than the indifference curve passing through his initial endowment is excluded. A final allocation like M' (see Fig. 6.1) is accordingly rejected since consumer 1 prefers his initial bundle $(a, 0)$ to the bundle M'. The set of acceptable allocations is thus reduced, by virtue of the first assumption, to those allocations falling between the indifference curves passing through initial endowments $(a, 0)$ and $(0, b)$. The second assumption serves to reduce the acceptable arrangements lying in this area to the tangent points between the two systems of indifference curves. Suppose, indeed, that a point such as M would be an acceptable arrangement. All allocations lying on indifference curves higher than those passing through M give both traders higher utility levels than those obtained at M: the allocation M is accordingly rejected by virtue of the second assumption. The only allocations which are not excluded by this reasoning are precisely those corresponding to a tangent point between two indifference curves. Any move from such a point implies that at least one trader loses utility as a consequence of this move. The set of allocations which satisfy simultaneously both the assumptions was referred to by Edgeworth as the *contract curve*. We notice that some allocations lying on the contract curve are more favourable to one trader than the other, while other allocations satisfy the reverse property: skill in bargaining will decide which, among these allocations, will finally obtain.

In the preceding analysis we have identified how cooperation leads to the selection of a particular class of outcomes in the simplest exchange context: two persons and two goods. Now we are ready to extend this approach to the general context of an exchange economy embodying an arbitrary number n of traders exchanging their initial endowments of goods. Denote by w_i the initial endowment of consumer i, $i = 1, ..., n$, a vector which has as many components as there are different commodities in the economy. The commodity bundle $\sum_{i=1}^{n} w_i$ denotes the total endowment of the economy. Now consider an allocation of this total endowment among the n consumers and denote by x_i the commodity bundle received by agent i from this allocation after exchange.

Let us then extend to this exchange context the same group rationality concept as that underlying the concept of the contract curve, but applied now to any group of traders, or *coalition*, which can be formed from the set of n traders participating in the exchange of goods: *an allocation will be rejected if there exists a coalition S of traders which can provide each of its members i with a commodity bundle y_i preferred to the commodity bundle x_i received from that allocation, using only its aggregate resources $\sum_{i \in S} w_i$*. The only allocations which remain acceptable as a final arrangement of exchange are those which are not rejected by any coalition. The set of these allocations is called *the core* of the exchange economy. The formal definition of the core is as follows. A coalition is a subset S of $(1, ..., n)$. A coalition S *improves upon* an allocation assigning x_i, $i = 1, ..., n$, to consumer i, when there exist commodity bundles y_i, $i \in S$, such that

$$\sum_{i \in S} y_i = \sum_{i \in S} w_i,$$

and y_i is preferred to x_i by each trader i belonging to the coalition S. The core is the set of allocations which cannot be improved upon by any coalition S. It is easy to verify that, in the case of two consumers and two goods, the core coincides with the contract curve.

6.1.2 *The core and the set of competitive allocations*

The concept of the core is defined independently of the price mechanism, while this is the mechanism which is generally considered in economics in order to characterize the allocation of goods among individuals. The mechanism underlying core allocations is direct exchange, without recourse to prices. The usual approach utilized by economists to describe the reallocation of commodities rests, however, on the existence of a *price system*, one price for each good, guaranteeing that supply equals demand on each particular market. More precisely, consumer i, initially endowed with the bundle w_i, maximizes his utility under a budget constraint guaranteeing that the value, at ongoing prices, of his purchases does not exceed the value, at the same prices, of his initial endowment of goods. This determines a demand vector for each consumer which, when aggregated over all consumers, defines the market demand at these prices. When the price constellation is such that aggregate supply equals aggregate demand on each market, this price constellation and the corresponding allocation of goods forms a *competitive equilibrium*. The term 'competitive', which qualifies this notion of equilibrium, comes from the fact that economic agents are supposed to evaluate their budget at *given* prices, thus behaving as price-takers. This notion of equilibrium thus translates the basic assumption of perfect competition. Economic agents do not perceive the interaction of their decisions when they select their market demands; it is through price adjustments that thousands of individual decisions, formulated independently from each other, are finally made compatible.

An interesting question is whether the two mechanisms – the core allocation mechanism and the price allocation mechanism – share some similarities in terms of the allocations which emerge from their functioning. In other words, can we compare the set of allocations in the core with the set of allocations which are competitive for a given exchange economy? At first sight, it seems difficult to expect such similarities, to the extent that the two concepts differ widely, the first relying on direct exchange while the second follows from price mediation. Surprisingly enough, core and competitive allocations are in fact very similar when the analysis is carried out at a deeper level.

First of all, *a competitive allocation is always in the core*. To prove this assertion, let us use an argument *ab absurdum*. Suppose that there exists a competitive allocation not belonging in the core. Then there exists a coalition S of traders which could distribute among its members, using only its own aggregate resources, $\sum_{i \in S} w_i$, commodity bundles which are preferred, by each of its members, to the bundle they receive at the competitive allocation being considered. But then the value of the former bundles is necessarily higher, at the competitive prices, than the value of their initial endowment for, otherwise, they would have selected in their budget set these bundles rather than the competitive bundles. But this implies that the value, at competitive prices, of the aggregate initial resources of the coalition exceeds the value, at the same prices, of the bundles distributed among the members of the coalition. This contradicts, however, the fact that the coalition has distributed these bundles on its own resources only.

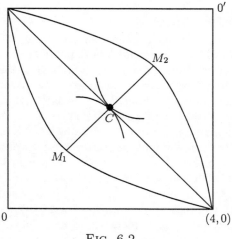

$$0$$
$$(4,0)$$

FIG. 6.2.

Furthermore, there exists a deeper relationship between the core and the set of competitive allocations, which is linked to the number of agents participating in the exchange process. To illustrate, let us consider again an Edgeworth box corresponding to an exchange situation involving two goods and two traders, with specific initial endowments and tastes. Agent 1 has an initial endowment $w_1 = (4,0)$ and agent 2 an initial endowment $w_2 = (0,4)$, so that each agent is a monopolist in his own good. Furthermore, the box is a square (see Fig. 6.2). Both consumers have the same utility function for the two goods, namely $u(x,y) = \sqrt{x} + \sqrt{y}$. It is easily seen that indifference curves corresponding to this utility function are symmetric along the diagonal in the box and as depicted in Fig. 6.2.

Suppose that the consumers decide to exchange goods via a price system assigning the same price to each good, each consumer selecting the most preferred bundle in his budget set expressed in these prices. Then each of them selects the commodity bundle $C = (2,2)$ which lies on the same budget line as his initial endowment $w_i, i = 1, 2$. At the allocation C, demand is equal to supply for both goods. Furthermore, the indifference curves of both agents are tangential at C: accordingly, the allocation C belongs to the contract curve. Notice also that this allocation is the only competitive allocation of this exchange economy. Thus we conclude that, in this example, the set of competitive allocations is included in the contract curve.

On the other hand, consider the set of all allocations which are on the contract curve. It is easily seen from Fig. 6.2 that this set is delimited by the segment $M_1 M_2$ of the main diagonal, so that the contract curve includes many allocations which are not competitive: there is no reason why, in the case of two agents, the competitive allocation should play a particular role in the exchange process. Indeed, with two agents only, it is hardly credible that they would proceed to the exchange of goods taking prices as given, as postulated by the competitive assumption. Most probably they will try to influence the exchange mechanism so as to secure the most advantageous outcome for themselves on the contract curve. Competitive assumptions, in particular the assumption of price-taking behaviour, can be meaningful only when the number of participants is so large that none of them can have a significant influence on market prices. Outside this context, it must be expected that any change in supply or demand for any agent should have a significant impact on the exchange rates among goods. However, with numerous agents, individual moves in demand or supply will have a negligible consequence on equilibrium prices. Accordingly, the number of exchange participants plays a crucial role in justifying the concept of competitive equilibrium: the higher this number, the more legitimate the use of the price-taking assumption (we shall see later that this legitimacy may disappear when agents start to 'organize' collusive agreements among themselves).

Does there exist a similar connection between the notion of the core and the number of agents in the economy? Putting it in another way, is the core sensitive to an increase in the number of market participants? Remember that an allocation is in the core when there exists no coalition which can improve upon it. But a coalition is a subset of the set $(1, ..., n)$. Accordingly, to check whether a particular allocation is in the core of an economy including n agents, any possible combination of these n agents into subgroups should be examined, since any such combination constitutes a potential coalition capable of improving upon a particular allocation. Since an allocation is declared to be out of the core whenever such a coalition exists, the greater the number of coalitions, the smaller the core. Since the number of feasible coalitions clearly increases with the number n of participants, the size of the core decreases when this number increases. To illustrate this shrinking process, let us come back for a moment to the exchange economy defined above. In Fig. 6.2 the allocation M_1 assigning the commodity bundles $(1, 1)$ to consumer 1 and $(3, 3)$ to consumer 2 is in the core of the exchange economy embodying these two consumers. Now consider the exchange economy embodying four consumers which is obtained by duplicating the preceding economy, with two consumers similar to consumer 1 and two consumers similar to consumer 2:

$$w_{11} = w_{12} = (4, 0)$$
$$w_{21} = w_{22} = (0, 4)$$
$$U_i(x, y) = \sqrt{x} + \sqrt{y}, i = 1, ..., 4.$$

By convention, we call consumers 11 and 12 the 'consumers of type 1' and consumers 21 and 22 the 'consumers of type 2'. This new economy simply 'duplicates' the exchange economy considered at the start, with two agents of each type. First it should be clear that the competitive allocation is the same in the new and the old economy: it assigns $(2, 2)$ to each consumer and the price ratio is still equal to 1. At this price ratio, supply on each market (8 units) is equal to total demand. Now consider the core of the duplicated economy embodying four agents. As we shall see, it is not difficult to show that the allocation M_1, assigning $(1,1)$ to agents 11 and 12, and $(3,3)$ to agents 21 and 22, which was in the core of the economy before replication, no longer belongs to the core of the replicated economy. Let us show, indeed, that the coalition composed of agents 11, 12 and 21 can improve upon this allocation. To see this, assign the bundle $(\frac{5}{2}, \frac{1}{2})$ to agents 11 and 12, and the bundle $(3,3)$ to agent 21. The total amount of the two goods assigned to the members of the coalition is then $(8,4)$, which is exactly the amount the coalition initially owns. We notice, however, that $u(\frac{5}{2}, \frac{1}{2}) = \sqrt{\frac{5}{2}} + \sqrt{\frac{1}{2}} > \sqrt{1} + \sqrt{1} = u(1,1)$, so that both agents 11 and 12 strictly prefer the bundle $(\frac{5}{2}, \frac{1}{2})$ to the bundle $(1,1)$. Since consumer 21 receives $(3,3)$ in the redistribution among the members of the coalition, he is as well off at this redistribution than he was at the allocation M_1. Consequently, the coalition can improve upon that allocation, from which it follows that it no longer belongs to the core of the replicated economy: the increase in the number of agents has narrowed the core!

Now we can combine the above results in order to state the general property which relates the core of an exchange economy to the set of its competitive allocations. First, the set of competitive allocations is always included in the core, whatever the number n of replications of a given exchange economy. Furthermore, the core shrinks when the economy is replicated, in the sense that the core of the economy replicated n times is included in the core of the same economy replicated $(n-1)$ times only: as a function of the number of replications, the cores form a decreasing sequence of sets. This question is referred into the literature as 'the Edgeworth conjecture': does the sequence of cores converge exactly to the set of competitive allocations when the number n of replications of the economy tends to infinity? A positive answer to this question was given by Debreu and Scarf (1963): *the allocations which remain in the core for all n are necessarily competitive allocations.* Thus, when the number of traders becomes very large, each individual agent loses his power to influence the selection of a particular allocation, whether he acts alone or collectively by forming coalitions with others; he is as well off by optimizing his purchases at given prices since, in any case, he cannot expect in the core a better treatment than the competing one.

This remarkable result constitutes a fundamental justification for using the concept of competitive equilibrium in economies including a large number of economic agents. It establishes that, in such an economy, even when consumers are freely allowed consciously to influence the result of barter exchange, they have nothing to gain by doing so: in any case they will obtain exactly what they would obtain as price-takers in a competitive economy. As we shall see in the next section, the validity of this result depends, however, on two conditions: first, the initial ownership of each good must be spread among many consumers; second, collusive agreements, aiming at influencing the result of collective exchange, should be precluded. These two conditions deal with imperfect competition, and it is therefore important to examine how the core behaves when they are not fulfilled.

6.1.3 *The core and imperfect competition*

The notion of perfect competition rests on the prerequisite that consumers are so numerous that none of them can significantly influence exchange conditions. Outside this context, this notion has no meaning because there is no reason why agents should behave as price-takers when there are only a few of them. The notion of the core does not require such a prerequisite concerning the number of agents: it is as significant in an economy embodying two agents as in an economy with a large number of them. Only the *dimension* of the core is sensitive to this number: When this number increases, it increases simultaneously the number of coalitions, which prevents any allocation which is not competitive from belonging to the core for all replications of the economy. At the limit, the core and the set of competitive allocations are two equivalent concepts. This conclusion, which is perfectly valid for the general case, is no longer true, however, in two particular cases which, in spite of being somewhat special, are often observed in real market situations. In the first case, there are many buyers and sellers, but the ownership of one or several goods is concentrated in the hands of one or very few traders. The second case corresponds to an initial situation embodying a large mass of economic agents, but some of them organize among themselves with a view to substituting for their individual freedom a collective decision process tying all individuals belonging to the group.

Here we recognize structures which are now familiar to us in the context of partial analysis: oligopolistic structures in the first case, and collusive coordination in the second. We now examine how these structures can be analysed when using core theory and the exchange model. We start with the case of *monopoly*. When a single trader initially owns the total endowment of a particular good, the other traders cannot avoid being dependent on him if they want to obtain some units of this good through trade. It is most likely that, in such a case, there is no hope of reconstituting the conditions of perfect competition simply by increasing the number of traders, if this increase does not entail simultaneously a spreading of initial ownership of the monopolized good. We may, however, raise the following question: *To what extent does the existence of a monopoly affect the reallocation of the goods, compared with the competitive allocation which would necessarily have obtained in a hypothetical economy where the same quantity of the monopolized good had been spread among a large number of agents?* Thanks to the concept of the core, it is now possible to answer this question. We know, indeed, from the conclusions of the preceding section, that the competitive allocations of this hypothetical economy coincide with its core. It is thus sufficient to compare this core with the core of the economy including a monopolist, to identify the distortions created by its existence.

To illustrate the above, let us come back to the bilateral monopoly example introduced in the preceding section. There it was explained that the competitive allocation $C = (2,2)$ had no particular significance in this situation, in which there are only two traders proceeding to the exchange of goods. We also saw that, when the initial economy is duplicated, some allocations in the core of the initial economy (for instance, the allocation M_1) are no longer in the core of the duplicated economy. Now extend this replication procedure to any integer n, the economy E_n being related to the initial economy in the following way. The economy E_n embodies $2n$ consumers, with the first group of n consumers exactly identical to consumer 1 in the initial economy, and the last group of n consumers exactly identical to consumer 2 in the same economy; that is,

$$w_{1j} = (4,0); j = 1, ..., n$$
$$w_{2j} = (0,4); j = 1, ..., n$$
$$u_{1j}(x,y) = u_{2j}(x,y) = \sqrt{x} + \sqrt{y}, j = 1, ..., 2n.$$

By convention we identify agents $1j$, $j = 1, ..., n$, as agents of type 1, and agents $2j$, $j = 1, ..., n$, as agents of type 2. The economy described is simply the initial economy E_1 replicated n times. Since all agents of type 1 (or type 2) are identical, it is clear that the only competitive allocation of the economy E_n assigns the bundle $C = (2, 2)$ to all consumers. By the Debreu Scarf theorem stated above, *the cores of the economies E_n shrink to this sole allocation when n tends to infinity.* Notice, however, that the replication procedure which was used to enlarge the economy E_1 guarantees not only that the number of agents increases without limit, but also that the initial ownership of both goods is spread over a larger and larger set of agents in proportion as n increases.

Now consider an alternative procedure for enlarging the same initial bilateral monopoly situation, which no longer implies that ownership of both goods is spread among an increasing number of agents. The economy E'_n embodies $n + 1$ agents. The initial endowment of the n traders $1j$, $j = 1, ..., n$, remains unchanged, $w_{1j} = (4, 0)$, while the initial endowment of agent $n + 1$ is redefined as $w_{n+1} = (0, 4n)$. The economy E'_n is totally similar to the economy E_n except that only one consumer initially owns the total amount of good 2 existing in the economy! It is possible to show that the asymptotic behaviour of the core of the economies E'_n completely differs from that just observed in the case of the economies E_n (Gabszewicz 1970). While the core of the economies E_n tends with n to the competitive allocation, the core of the economies E'_n *tends to the set of allocations in the core of E_1, at which the utility of agent $n + 1$ exceeds the utility of this agent at the competitive allocation. At the limit, only those allocations on the segment M_1C remain in the core for all n* (see Fig. 6.2). At these allocations, the monopolist can still exploit the agents of type 1 in the sense that he can get more in utility than at the competitive outcome. By contrast, this possibility is no longer open to the latter agents, since in any case the former gets *at least* his competitive payoff! In the extreme case just described, it is thus possible to identify precisely the distortion in the set of core allocations due to the presence of a monopolist. For large values of n, while only the competitive allocation would obtain in the core when the initial ownership of both goods is adequately spread, monopoly generates possibilities of exploitation in the core in favour of the monopolist, compared with his utility at the competitive solution.

The second situation of imperfect competition evoked at the beginning of this section concerns group formation among consumers on the basis of collusive behaviour. It is not possible, in the framework of this introductory book, to provide a detailed analysis of core theory contributions to the study of this question. Nevertheless, I would like to suggest briefly how the analysis of collusion can be tackled in general equilibrium using the concept of core. To this end, consider again the economy E_n for large values of n. In this economy, *when all coalitions may freely be formed*, only the competitive allocation C remains robust against the possibility for any coalition to improve upon a proposed reallocation of goods among the consumers. But now suppose that, in the economy E_n, all agents of type 2 decide to form a 'syndicate' of the owners of good 2, and delegate to one of them the power of negotiating the exchange of good 2 against good 1 with the agents of type 1. Then the economy E_n is transformed into a new economy which is exactly the same as the economy E'_n considered above, including a monopolist of good 2: the agent delegated by the syndicate is now the monopolist! Consequently, *after* the syndicate has formed, the core is enlarged to the whole segment M_1C (see Fig. 6.2), exactly as in the case of monopoly analysed above. By delegating its power to a single agent, the syndicate has succeeded in erasing all coalitions including a proper subset of type 2 agents, coalitions which would otherwise have improved upon any allocation which was not competitive! Accordingly, by forming 'pressure groups', agents can countervail the dilution of their individual power resulting from the large number of decision units participating in the economy. Thanks to collusion, the members of the syndicate integrate into one decision unit their individual strengths which were initially separated and, accordingly, diluted. They are able to restore monopoly , whereas they would otherwise have obtained their competitive outcome as a result of their *initial* competing position. Of course, this situation is akin of the one encountered on the corn market of Chapter 2, where all the producers of this commodity were able, thanks to a collusive agreement, to substitute the monopoly solution to the competitive one. The progress made follows from the fact that we have analysed here the same phenomenon, but in a general equilibrium model. In the next section, we proceed in the same spirit by proposing an extension of non-cooperative Cournot analysis, formulated in Chapter 2 in a partial equilibrium model, to the general equilibrium context of a pure exchange economy.

6.2 The non-cooperative approach

The cooperative theory of exchange based on the concept of the core has made possible an analysis of how ownership asymmetries or collusive behaviour of the agents may alter the exchange mechanism, compared with that observed on competitive exchange markets obeying price decentralization. In this section, we will proceed in an analogous manner, assuming here that the agents exerting power on exchange behave non-cooperatively. We hope thereby to show that the Cournot equilibrium concept, introduced for the analysis of a single market, extends easily to the context of a system of interrelated markets. Again, we limit ourselves to the context of pure exchange.

Consider again, as at the end of the preceding section, an exchange situation in which the ownership of some good is concentrated in the hands of a few agents – we call them the *oligopolists* – while the initial ownership of the other goods is spread among a large number of different agents: we call the latter the *competitive sector*. Furthermore, we suppose that exchange takes place at those prices for which supply is equal to demand on every market, the equilibrium prices. However, and contrary to the assumption leading to a competitive allocation, we shall assume that, far from taking prices as given, oligopolists try to manipulate them to their advantage, in a non-cooperative manner. By contrast, the agents in the competitive sector are assumed to behave as price-takers.

In order to introduce a notion of non-cooperative equilibrium in a way analogous to Cournot, let us consider an exchange economy in which the total endowment of good 1 belongs initially to the oligopolists, while the endowment of the other goods is initially dispersed among the agents in the competitive sector. Exchange takes place in the following way. First each oligopolist selects the quantity of the good he owns initially which he is willing to sell on the market for good 1, knowing that his *final* endowment in that good will be equal to the difference between what he owns initially and what he has decided to sell. It follows that the income of each oligopolist is equal to the amount sold of good 1 times the price of good 1. With this income he buys, at given prices, a preferred bundle of the other goods, owned by the competitive sector, on the corresponding markets. Under the assumption that the agents in the competitive sector behave as price-takers on *all* markets, there exists an excess demand function for each good (where excess demand is defined as the difference between the total quantity demanded of a good and the total endowment of it in the economy) *except on the market for good 1*. On this market, excess demand appears as the difference between total demand of the competitive sector for that good and *the aggregate supply decided by the oligopolists*.

Then consider the price system which clears all markets, the market for good 1 included. It is clear that the clearing price on this market, and accordingly the clearing prices on all markets, will depend on the amount of good 1 which has been selected for sale by each individual oligopolist. Consequently, each oligopolist exerts a partial control on equilibrium prices, by manipulating the fraction of his initial holdings of good 1 which he decides to send to the market for exchange: each oligopolist faces a price function depending in particular on his own supply strategy, but also on the supply strategies of the others. Accordingly, oligopolists' strategies are interrelated through the price function just described. We recognize the context of interactive decision-making which we analysed in the preceding chapters, but formulated now in a general equilibrium approach.

To illustrate the notion of equilibrium derived in this context, let us define the following exchange economy including two goods and $n + 2$ consumers. All consumers have the same utility function defined by $u(x^1, x^2) = x^1 x^2$. As for the initial endowments, they are defined as follows:

$$w_i = (1,0), \quad i = 1,2$$
$$w_i = (0, 1/n), \, i = 3, ..., n+2.$$

Thus initial holdings of good 1 belong to the 'duopolists' 1 and 2, while the ownership of good 2 is dispersed among the agents $3, ..., n + 2$, belonging to the competitive sector (n is assumed to be large). By definition, a *strategy* for duopolist $i, i = 1, 2$, is a number e_i belonging to the interval $(0, 1)$: the quantity e_i expresses the amount of good 1 that duopolist i decides to send to the market for sale through which he may manipulate the exchange rate between good 1 and good 2. Let p denote the price for good 1 and set the price of good 2 equal to 1, which is equivalent to using good 2 as a numeraire. The demand for the two goods emanating from the competitive sector is obtained by maximizing the utility $x^1 x^2$ of each consumer in this sector under the budget constraint $px^1 + x^2 = \frac{1}{n}$: recall that these agents behave as price-takers on both markets. The solution to this maximization problem gives $(\frac{1}{2}pn, \frac{1}{2}n)$ as the individual demand vector for each agent in the competitive sector so that the aggregate demand for good 1 at price p is equal to $\frac{1}{2p}$. Furthermore, if e_1 and e_2 are the quantities supplied by the duopolists 1 and 2, respectively, the price $p(e_1, e_2)$ which equates supply and demand for good 1 must satisfy the equality

$$\frac{1}{2p(e_1, e_2)} = e_1 + e_2,$$

so that

$$p(e_1, e_2) = \frac{1}{2(e_1 + e_2)}.$$

Consequently, the utility obtained by duopolist 1 when using strategy e_1 is given by $(1 - e_1)\frac{e_1}{2(e_1+e_2)}$: the first term of this product is equal to the amount of good 1 still available for consumption after sending e_1 to the market, while the second term is equal to the amount of good 2 he can buy at price $p(e_1, e_2)$ taking into account his budget constraint. An analogous reasoning shows that the utility obtained by the second oligopolist using the strategy e_2 obtains as $(1 - e_2)\frac{e_2}{2(e_1+e_2)}$. Now recall that a non-cooperative equilibrium is a pair of strategies (e_1^*, e_2^*) such that no unilateral deviation from it can increase the payoff of a player. In other words, the non-cooperative equilibrium is given by the simultaneous solution of the following two problems:

$$\max_{e_1 \in [0,1]} (1 - e_1)\frac{e_1}{2(e_1 + e_2)}$$

and

$$\max_{e_2 \in [0,1]} (1 - e_2)\frac{e_2}{e(e_1 + e_2)}.$$

The first-order necessary conditions give the linear system

$$e_2 - e_{12} - 2e_1e_2 = 0$$
$$e_1 - e_{22} - 2e_1e_2 = 0.$$

Since payoffs are symmetric, we may solve this system by setting $e_1 = e_2$, which gives $e_1^* = e_2^* = \frac{1}{3}$, to which corresponds the equilibrium price $p(e_1^*, e_2^*) = \frac{3}{4}$. At this price, each duopolist obtains the bundle $(\frac{2}{3}, \frac{1}{4})$, and each consumer in the competitive sector the bundle $(\frac{2}{3}n, \frac{1}{2}n)$.

It is interesting to compare the oligopolistic solution just described with the solution which would obtain if all agents had behaved competitively, including the duopolists. In this case they also take the prices as given, without manipulating them via their supply of good 1. A simple calculation shows that the competitive allocation is then given by the bundles $(\frac{1}{2}, \frac{1}{4})$ for consumers 1 and 2, and $(\frac{1}{n}, \frac{1}{2n})$ for consumers in the competitive sector. The equilibrium exchange rate is given by $p = \frac{1}{2}$. Thus we notice that, by manipulating the equilibrium price $p(e_1, e_2)$, the duopolists have succeeded in obtaining as much of good 2 as at the competitive outcome, but by selling less of good 1 (at the competitive allocation, they sell a half-unit of this good, while they sell only one-third as duopolists). This profit has been made possible because, even without cooperation, they obtain a more favourable exchange rate for their good thanks to the fact that both of them restrict their supply of it at equilibrium, compared with their competitive supply.

On the other hand, we could easily consider the same example, but assuming now that not two, but m oligopolists share the ownership of commodity 1. Calculating the corresponding oligopolistic solution, as we did for the case of duopoly, we would show that this solution converges to the competitive solution we have just identified, when the number m of oligopolists tends to infinity. We rediscover here a result familiar to us in the context of partial equilibrium: free entry makes the market power of each agent negligible when the number of agents increases without limit (see Codognato and Gabszewicz 1991).

7

CONCLUSION

This monograph has illustrated how theorists have analysed situations in which the assumptions underlying the perfectly competitive paradigm no longer hold. Having come this far, one cannot avoid some scepticism. Contrary to the theory of perfectly competitive markets, the theoretical approach to imperfect competition suffers from a lack of unity, and resembles a colourful patchwork, made of the juxtaposition of specific models, which contrasts with the beautiful harmony of the competitve world.

A good example of this peculiarity is provided by the Hotelling model of spatial competition. In spite of its ingeniousness, this analysis does not lead to a clear and *general* conclusion concerning the degree of product differentiation: when transportation costs are linear in distance, firms prefer to reduce the distance which separates them, while the reverse conclusion holds when costs are quadratic! We could quote several other examples of models specially built to explain specific market circumstances, but with conclusions as fragile as the specifications for which they are shown to be valid.

Beyond the problem of theoretical fragmentation induced by the multiplicity of specific models, the analysis of imperfect competition also suffers from a difficulty shared by several approaches using game theory: either there is no equilibrium, or there are too many! Thus, for instance, there exists no non-cooperative equilibrium in Hotelling's model with linear transportation costs when firms are located too close to each other (see Chapter 4). By contrast, equilibria can proliferate in other situations, and it is difficult to select among them the most 'significant' for the analysis. The first difficulty has been circumvented by introducing the so-called *mixed* strategies. A mixed strategy is a random choice mechanism bearing on the set of the so-called 'pure' strategies: instead of selecting a particular strategy with probability one (which is the case for a pure strategy), each pure strategy is weighted by a probability which represents the likelihood of being selected by the decision-maker. The extension of the strategy sets to the use of mixed strategies often provides the existence of an equilibrium in mixed strategies, while no equilibrium exists when the game is restricted to pure strategies. This procedure is a *deus ex machina* which is not really convincing because it is not easy to interpret the economic significance of a mixed strategy. Furthermore, the use of mixed strategies is hardly ever observed in the real world. To palliate the abundance of equilibria when there are too many of them, game theorists have proposed 'refinement mechanisms' which select, among equilibria, some of those which satisfy more restrictive properties.

Leaving aside the complexity of these mechanisms, their interpretation is often difficult and ambiguous.

The above comments thus exhibit some methodological reservations on the theoretical approaches adopted when analysing imperfectly competitive markets. But it is important to recall that perfect competition, whose theoretical representation does not entail similar criticisms, constitutes an extremely particular case of market reality: economic agents are *assumed* from the outset to exert no market power. *Imperfect* competition is accordingly meant to take care of all alternative forms of markets, and it must not be expected that a unique theoretical model could represent all the alternative possibilities. Furthermore, the consequences of strategic interaction are particularly sensitive to the characteristics of firms in terms of their products, their costs and the information which is available to the agents. Accordingly, it is not surprising that many models are introduced in order to study the implications of these specific characteristics in various environments.

Most of market situations analysed in this monograph deal with strategic interaction among firms resulting from the interdependence of *demand* for products. In particular, the 'market power' of the agents generally comes from their ability to influence the market price, and consequently the quantity demanded, either because firms have the power to set the price themselves, or because they manipulate the price through the quantity supplied. In reality, however, market power often originates in the *technological conditions* under which firms realize their products. Then imperfect competition comes from the *supply* conditions. More precisely, the existence of increasing returns to scale prevents the possibility for several firms to realize each strictly positive profits, thereby forcing the survival of only a small number of firms (the extreme case corresponding to this case is the natural monopoly situation which was mentioned in Chapter 2). These firms are then automatically placed in a context of strategic interaction, often made more complex because of sequential entry. Although theorists have tried to study these situations (limit pricing theory is one of them), it must be recognized that their efforts have not be very successful. Increasing returns to scale, combined with dynamic entry processes, prevent a satisfactory explanation of how the long-run equilibrium obtains, and of the number of firms which will be active at such an equilibrium.

Furthermore, the analysis of imperfect competition has not solved one of the major questions of micro theory: how are prices formed? Of course, several of the approaches included in this book allow firms to quote their prices, which then appear as strategic variables to them. This clearly constitutes progress, compared with the assumption of the 'Walrasian auctioneer' coordinating sellers' and buyers' decisions. But quantity models, like that of Cournot, still persist in assuming implicitly the existence of an auctioneer calculating the price at which sellers' and buyers' decisions are compatible. This assumption circumvents the difficulty of representing how market operators coordinate their decisions through a myriad of bilateral contracts made by different buyers and sellers. In particular, theory is unable to explain how the simple fact that there is only a small number of agents simplifies this coordination problem, when compared with its complexity under perfect competition in which a large number of agents is postulated from the outset.

In conclusion, the theories presented above suffer from several inadequacies. Not only do they form a conglomerate of specific models, but often they fail to produce an equilibrium. Furthermore, they are unable to answer several questions which appear to be crucial to the understanding of the operation of markets, such as the role of increasing returns to scale or the manner in which individual decisions are coordinated by price mediation. But, in spite of these drawbacks, they at least have the merit of drawing the attention of economists to the importance of abandoning the competitive paradigm in favour of a more realistic approach to markets.

REFERENCES

Akerlof, G. (1970). The market for lemons: Quality uncertainty and the market mechanism. *Quarterly Journal of Economics*, **84**, 777–95.

Alchian, A. and W. Allen (1972). *University Economics*. Wadswroth Publishing Company, Belmont.

Benassy, J.P. (1991). Optimal government policy in a macroeconomic model with Imperfect competition and rational expectations. In W. Barnett *et al.* (eds), *Equilibrium Theory and Applications*, pp. 339–52. Cambridge University Press, Cambridge.

Bertrand, J. (1883). Revue de recherches sur les principes mathématiques de la théorie des richesses de Cournot. *Journal des Savants*, 499–508.

Chamberlin, E. (1933). *The Theory of Monopolistic Competition*. Harvard University Press, Cambridge, MA.

Codognato, G. and J. Gabszewicz (1991). Equilibres de Cournot-Walras dans une économie d'échange. *Revue économique*, **42**, 1013–26.

Cournot, A. (1838). *Recherches sur les principes mathématiques de la théorie des richesses*. (New edition 1974.) Calmann-Levy, Paris.

d'Aspremont, C., Gabszewicz, J. and J. Thisse (1979). On Hotelling's stability in competition. *Econometrica*, **47**, 1145–50.

d'Aspremont, C., Jacquemin, A., Gabszewicz, J. and J. Weymark (1983). On the stability of collusive price leadership. *Canadian Journal of Economics*, **14**, 17–25.

d'Aspremont, C., Dos Santos Ferreira, R. and L.-A. Gérard-Varet (1991). Imperfect competition, rational expectations, and unemployment. In W. Barnett *et al.* (eds), *Equilibrium Theory and Applications*. Cambridge University Press, Cambridge.

Debreu, G. (1959). *Theory of Value*. Wiley, New York.

de Fraja, G. and F. Delbono (1989). Game-theoretic models of mixed oligopoly. *Journal of Economic Surveys*, **4**, 1–17.

Dixit, A. (1980). The role of investment in entry-deterrence. *Economic Journal*, **90**, 95–106.

Eaton, B. and R. Lipsey (1978). Freedom of entry and the existence of pure profits. *Economic Journal*, **88**, 455–69.

Edgeworth, F. (1881). *Mathematical Psychics*. Kegan Paul, London.

Friedman, J. (1983). *Oligopoly Theory*, Cambridge University Press, Cambridge.

Gabszewicz, J. (1970). Théorie du noyau et de la concurrence imparfaite. *Recherches économiques de Louvain*, **36**, 21–37.

Gabszewicz, J. and P. Garella (1986). Subjective price search and price competition. *International Journal of Industrial Organization*, **4**, 306–15.

Gabszewicz, J. and I. Grilo (1992). Price competition when consumers are uncertain about which firm sells which quality. *Journal of Economics and Management Strategy*, **1**, 629–50.

Gabszewicz, J. and J. Thisse (1979). Price competition, quality and income disparities. *Journal of Economic Theory*, **20**, 340–59.

Gaskins, D. (1971). Dynamic limit pricing: Optimal pricing under threat of entry. *Journal of Economic Theory*, **3**, 306–22.

Grilo, I. (1994). Mixed duopoly under vertical differentiation. *Annales d'Economie et de Statistique*, **33**, 91–112.

Helpman, E. and G. Krugman (1986). *Market Structure and Foreign Trade*. Harvester Press.

Hotelling, H. (1929). Stability in competition. *Economic Journal*, **39**, 41–57.

Kreps, D. and J. Scheinkman (1983). Quantity precommitment and Bertrand competition yield Cournot outcomes. *Bell Journal of Economics*, **14**, 326–37.

Lancaster, K. (1966). A new approach to consumer theory. *Journal of Political Economy*, **74**, 132–157.

Ross, S. (1973). The economic theory of agency: The principal's problem. *American Economic Review*, **63**, 134–9.

Rothschild, M. and J. Stiglitz (1976). Equilibrium in competitive insurance markets: An essay on the economics of Imperfect competition. *Quarterly Journal of Economics*, **91**, 629–50.

Scherer, F. (1979) *Industrial Market Structures and Economic Performance* (2nd edn). Rand McNally, New York.

Schumpeter, J. (1954). *History of Economic Analysis*. Allen & Unwin, London.

Shaked, A. and J. Sutton (1983). Natural oligopolies. *Econometrica*, **51**, 1469–83.

Spence, M. (1974). *Market Signaling*. Harvard University Press, Cambridge, MA.

Stigler, G.J. (1950). Monopoly and oligopoly by merger. *American Economic Review*, 'Papers and Proceedings', **40**, 23–34.

Stigler, G.J. (1961) The economics of information. *Journal of Political Economy*, **69**, 213–25.

Stiglitz, J. (1989). Imperfect information in the product market. In R. Schmalensee and R. Willig (eds), *Handbook of Industrial Organization*, Volume 1, Chapter 13. North-Holland, Amsterdam.

Sylos Labini, P. (1957). *Oligopolio e Progresso Tecnico*. Giuffrè, Milan.

Tirole, J. (1988). *The Theory of Industrial Organization*. MIT Press, Cambridge.

Varian, H. (1993). *Intermediate Microeconomics* (3rd edn). W.W. Norton, New York.

von Neumann, J. and O. Morgenstern (1945). *Theory of Games and Economic Behaviour*. Princeton University Press, Princeton, NJ.

INDEX